High Schools as Communities:
The Small School Reconsidered

by
Thomas B. Gregory
and
Gerald R. Smith

Phi Delta Kappa Educational Foundation
Bloomington, Indiana

Cover design by Peg Caudell

Library of Congress Catalog Card Number 86-61933
ISBN 0-87367-433-2
Copyright © 1987 by Thomas B. Gregory and Gerald R. Smith
Printed in the United States of America

Dedication

To the teachers and their students in small high schools throughout the country, who have shown us the potential of community, this book is gratefully dedicated.

Acknowledgments

In thanking those who have contributed in very significant ways to the shaping of this book, there is the danger of omitting others who are equally deserving of recognition. We will risk it.

We would like to thank Arnie Langberg and the staff and students of Jefferson County Open High School for allowing us to visit and then describe their wonderful school in so public a forum. They provided numerous documents that helped us build an accurate description of the school's program. Their reactions to various drafts of Chapter 6 were very valuable. One of the documents the school provided us was Bert Horwood's ethnography of the school. It is an extremely rich description of the life of the school, and we thank Bert for allowing us to quote from it extensively. Mary Ellen Sweeney provided chapters from her study of the school, and we thank her for allowing us to quote a number of passages.

We also wish to thank the two schools described in Chapter 2. We cannot acknowledge their contribution to the book more directly because of our commitment to protect their anonymity. For a very intense week, they allowed us to peek into all their affairs and to ask many difficult and embarrassing questions. We appreciate their commitment to truth and their willingness to reveal not only their significant successes but also their warts.

Our secretaries deserve much credit. Jan Torgerson accomplished the difficult task of transcribing many hours of taped interviews. Roberta Van Pelt and Debbie Woodward suffered the onerous task of deciphering our terrible handwriting and transforming it into machine-readable files. We also thank them for the many times they "covered" for us, in one way or another, as we occasionally neglected duties to work on the book.

On several occasions, we had trouble recalling exactly where we had read an idea we were using. Anne Lentz brought her considerable library skills to bear in tracking down the most elusive of our citations.

We thank our families for putting up with their distracted husbands/fathers. We are not sure which of two outcomes would have ensued without them: the book might never have been finished at all; or equally probable, it might have been finished several months earlier.

And we wish to thank the teachers and students who welcomed us into their schools and patiently helped us to understand the significance of their efforts. Without them, the book never would have been conceived.

Table of Contents

Snapshots

We are in a colonial American history (not "social studies") class at a small high school in Colorado. The room is abuzz with individual and small group activity. Students are poring over old *National Geographics*, thumbing through history books, consulting road maps, and typing letters. The class is preparing for an 18-day, 7,000-mile trip through colonial America, first to Boston, then to Virginia, and finally returning home.

The students are arranging places to stay — mostly in the homes of other high school students — deciding what to see, organizing fund-raising projects, and deciding what food and supplies they should take. The teacher is stationed at his desk in a corner of the room, functioning as a resource person for anyone that needs help. Few do. We complimented him for undertaking this ambitious project. He responded by telling us that this will be a pared-down version of the trip taken by the previous year's class, which traveled all the way to St. Augustine, Florida, studying the same topic.

We were impressed by how matter-of-factly he viewed the whole endeavor; the logistics and liability issues alone boggled our minds. We understood better later in the day, when another teacher commented about how important travel had become in the curriculum of this school but told us the trip she and her students were planning this term fell through. It was simply going to cost too much to go to China!

* * *

In a small high school in Utah, all the students are either already teenage mothers or are about to have babies. The students have formed a discussion circle. A few hold babies on their laps; two babies play on blankets in the center of the circle. Occasionally a young woman recognizes a cry from the nursery down the hall as coming from her baby, and she leaves to attend to its needs.

The class is discussing the state law that limits sex education. They particularly are concerned about existing prohibitions against schools disseminating birth-control information and see their current circumstances to be due in part to such restrictions. Their teacher asks the students what they would like to do. They could write to each state legislator; they could go to Salt Lake City to talk to the law-makers directly. Who these young women are — unwed mothers — would speak as loudly for new legislation as what they had to say.

The teacher asks if they understand the concept of lobbying and what they could do to be a more effective lobby for their issue. They should become well-informed about the history of sex-education laws in Utah; they need to understand the law-making process; they have to know who are the key people for and against such laws. They decide to prepare their case, plan their strategy, travel to the capital, and make their argument directly to the legislature.

* * *

At another small high school in Colorado, a hearing is being conducted by an *ad hoc* panel of three students and two teachers. During the return trip from an off-campus activity, a student in the back of the bus had allegedly displayed, but apparently had not smoked, a marijuana "joint." The action is a serious breach of school rules; the teacher in charge called for a "hearing," the process this school uses to deal with all significant infractions of rules.

The student majority on the hearing panel is designed to communicate to students that they have significant power and must exercise a commensurate responsibility for maintaining order in this school. The defendant and accuser each ask one student and one teacher to sit on the panel. The third "neutral" student is picked by teachers not directly involved in the incident.

The panel convenes immediately in the school library. Each side presents its witnesses and evidence. Panel members ask a number of questions. After hearing all the evidence, the panel withdraws to decide the case. The verdict: a recommendation for a three-day suspension from school is forwarded to the principal.

Later, the teachers involved conduct a post-mortem of the hearing. The evidence, in their view, had been convincing. They conclude that the punishment had been too light. They note that the "neutral" student panel member was too close a friend of the defendant to be unbiased in such a hearing. Of interest to us is that at no time in the lengthy, sometimes heated conversation do any of these teachers find fault with the hearing process itself. They are committed to the process even when, in their view, the outcome is less than satisfactory.

* * *

We are relaxing with the principal of a small high school in an Eastern state and discussing the school's image in the community. The students are free to govern their own time when they do not have a class. What is viewed by the school as a significant opportunity for learning to use time productively and responsibly is viewed by the community as undue permissiveness. Indeed, the school is known in the community as "a school for druggies and dropouts."

Based on our brief experience with the school, the descriptor seems grossly unfair. We ask the principal what the school has done to alter its image. He says that the staff and students have tried a number of things, but nothing seems very effective. We ask if the school district collects any achievement data that might be employed to alter the prevailing sentiment. He answers that the state periodically conducts evaluations of all schools and that this school came off "very well" on that collection of 14 cognitive and affective measures. This little school for druggies and dropouts has scored at the 99th percentile in the entire state on 13 of the 14 measures. It scored only at the 90th percentile on the 14th measure.

* * *

These school snapshots share a number of common characteristics. The incidents described all happened in U.S. public high schools; none describes an elite, private institution that caters to the best prepared of America's students. These schools have evolved very different programs within the constraints of existing district policies and funding levels. They all employ certified teachers trained in essentially the same manner in which all teachers are trained. None has more than a typi-

3

cal proportion of highly gifted or talented students nor, we might add, more than a typical proportion of similarly endowed teachers. Indeed, some have student populations comprised primarily of other high schools' unwanted, "problem" students. They all are relatively new schools, the oldest being less than 15 years old. They all are small schools, the largest having a few more than 200 students. And most important, they all have made a conscious decision to develop new ways of educating their students.

In part because of their small size and in part because of conscious efforts to do so, they all have developed cultures that differ greatly from the typical American high school. They have a very strong sense of community; and because of this sense of community, these schools are able to function in ways very different from the typical, large American high school. They have different organizational structures requiring different roles for students and teachers, and they offer programs that transcend classroom walls and textbook covers.

The typical American high school, according to a number of recent national reports, is in serious trouble. The precise nature of the problems is widely debated. But the solutions that have been proposed assume reforms will take place in the existing large physical facilities that have been built over the years. This book is our attempt to challenge that assumption and to investigate alternatives for what is socially, economically, and politically possible with regard to American high schools. To accomplish this goal we shall describe our experiences with a collection of thriving public high schools — schools that are succeeding where so many others are foundering, not because they have "solved" the problems of the American high school, but because they have been designed in ways that render these problems irrelevant or at least less intractable.

Experiencing such schools is a revelation. They have much to teach us. Our own experience with these schools has prompted us to construct the nine-point argument that is the basis for this book:

- The high school has become a fundamentally flawed institution. Designed for our grandparents and essentially unchanged since, it has gradually lost the support of large segments of the populace it is supposed to serve.
- High schools have not worked well for students for some time. The current perception of a crisis is that high schools no longer work well for teachers as well.

4

- The large size of the high school, once considered its strength, has become its major handicap. It has become a difficult institution for people to commit to or identify with.
- In contrast, a collection of public high schools, designed in the past decade and a half for today's youth, have developed markedly superior social climates without sacrificing achievement.
- These high schools differ from one another on many dimensions. What they have in common is a small student population, the largest having only 200 to 250 students.
- What seems most critical is not only the small number of students but also the small number of teachers, who enjoy a sense of professional autonomy and efficacy long absent from most larger high schools.
- By broadening definitions of how an education is delivered to students, who may deliver it, and where it may occur, these small high schools do not compromise the quality of the programs they offer.
- These schools need not cost more money. Most of them operate under the same funding formulas imposed on other high schools in their districts. Their structure generally enables them to convert significant portions of the overhead costs of a large institution into direct instruction.
- Their small size means that these schools serve only a small community. Yet, because these small schools are purposefully different from each other, they expand the educational options of the populace they serve within the public sector.

These nine points may not be evident in the structure of the book, but we address all of them, roughly in the order in which they are presented here. We begin in the next chapter with a critique of what prominent authorities are saying about today's high school.

Chapter 1
The Reformers Look at Schools Again

> *American schools are in trouble. In fact, the problems of schooling are of such crippling proportions that many schools may not survive. It is possible that our entire public education system is nearing collapse. We will continue to have schools, no doubt, but the basis of their support and their relationships to families, communities, and states could be quite different from what we have known.*
>
> —John Goodlad (1984, p. 1)

For the sixth time in four decades, we have been told that the high school is in trouble. In the early Fifties, a handful of critics, Athur Bestor most notable among them, lamented what Progressive Education had wrought. The fiery rhetoric was portrayed in such titles as *Educational Wastelands* (Bestor 1953), *And Madly Teach* (Smith 1949), *Quackery in the Public Schools* (Lynd 1953), and *Why Johnny Can't Read* (Flesch 1955).

Sputnik's launch in 1957 stimulated a second round of criticism. America had fallen behind the Soviet Union, particularly in math and the sciences; and this "national crisis" was met with considerable federal funds and a spate of alphabet-soup curriculum projects (SMSG math, BSCS biology, and PSSC physics, to name a few).

Next came all the discussion surrounding the Coleman Report of 1966. James Coleman shook many assumptions about what was required to improve education. More money alone did not produce better education.

In the late Sixties, the works of such "romantic critics" as Herbert Kohl, Jonathan Kozol, James Herndon, and John Holt, capped by Charles Silberman's *Crisis in the Classroom* (1970), formed a fourth round of criticism. These critics argued that the schools were mindless institutions that brutalized both the young and their teachers and warped learning beyond recognition.

Following closely on the heels of the romantic critics was a fifth round of studies and commission reports including the report of the National Commission on the Reform of Secondary Education (1973), the report of the subcommittee of the United States Senate's Judiciary Committee, *Our Nation's Schools — A Report Card* (1975), and *The Greening of the High School* (Weinstock 1973). These reports often recommended alternative high schools either directly or indirectly. Because of these recommendations, hundreds of public alternative high schools were started.

It is in the ebb and flow of this recurring criticism that the most recent round of reports, mostly critical of the high school, is grounded. Five of these recent reports characterize the range of current comment about America's public high schools. These five share little in common beyond that generalization.

Three of the five have shaped much of the public discussion about schools. The shortest of these also contains the most inflammatory rhetoric. *A Nation at Risk: The Imperative for Educational Reform,* the report of the National Commission on Excellence in Education (1983), is seasoned with such quotable phrases as, "If an unfriendly power had attempted to impose on America the mediocre educational performance that exists today, we might well have viewed it as an act of war" (p. 5). This report, widely discussed in the news media, generated much heat but little light. Its primary role may have been to arouse political activity, to prod state legislatures and school boards into action.

Ernest Boyer's *High School: A Report on Secondary Education in America* (1983), the report of a three-year study by the Carnegie Foundation for the Advancement of Teaching, examines 15 representative public high schools. According to Boyer, the institution of the high school is fundamentally sound; and much of the book is a call for a return to what once worked well in the high school.

Perhaps the most empathic of the five is Theodore Sizer's *Horace's Compromise: The Dilemma of the American High School* (1984).

Sizer portrays the difficulties of functioning effectively as either a student or a teacher in an institution badly stretched by society's many conflicting demands. He calls for decentralizing the high school into smaller, more manageable, less bureaucratic entities.

The last two books in our list are not as well known. Both are careful analyses that, in successive years, received the American Educational Research Association's Outstanding Book Award. Sara Lawrence Lightfoot's *The Good High School: Portraits of Character and Culture* (1983) looks at six high schools in three highly contrasting socioeconomic settings that, in her judgment, all work well. In this sense, the book serves as a foil to the harshness of *A Nation at Risk*. John Goodlad's *A Place Called School: Prospects for the Future* (1984), a study of 38 schools including 12 high schools, is perhaps the most balanced, comprehensive presentation among these five and calls for a redesign of the institution.

That these five books can study the same institution and draw such varying conclusions is of more than academic interest. The high school is asked to accomplish so many things that two observers with very different, but equally "valid" expectations can see much "goodness" as Lightfoot does or much disarray as the National Commission on Excellence in Education does.

Of particular interest to us are the views these five analyses present of six aspects of the American high school: 1) students and the act of learning; 2) teachers and the act of teaching; 3) the role of students, teachers, and parents in the governance of the school; 4) the school's program; 5) the structure or organization of the high school; and 6) its social climate or sense of community. These six factors encompass most of the forces that define what has been called the culture of the high school; and that culture's resistance to change has stimulated much of the continuous stream of criticism outlined above. That these five works can so clearly berate the high school's atrophy and, at the same time, so willingly accept its current culture as a given is, in our view, a major incongruity. Indeed, we contend that culture, by its pervasive nature, is the key to any reform strategy for the American high school.

Students and the Act of Learning

These five books offer a wide range of views of students and learning. Sizer, by far, presents the most complete statement on these topics. At the core of his recommendations is the need to understand the par-

8

ticular needs, vulnerabilities, and motivations of adolescents. Learning needs to be a conscious act, and schools must allow latitude for the sort of experimentation that results in personalized learning. Students need more autonomy if they are to take their learning seriously, and depth of learning should take precedence over breadth of content. But because Sizer says little about where learning should take place, we must assume that he expects it to occur mostly in classrooms. However, when writing about vocational education, Sizer states, "The best place to learn most jobs in on site" (p. 135).

The assumption that learning occurs primarily in classrooms also seems to underlie much of Goodlad's book. This constraint comes through clearly when he says, "We will only begin to get evidence of the potential power of pedagogy when we dare to risk and support markedly deviant *classroom* procedures" (p. 249, emphasis added). Goodlad would probably acknowledge that students can learn in a variety of settings, but his thinking still is focused on a single setting: the classroom.

For Goodlad, learning is tied to personal development; it must distinguish the mere acquisition of facts from the deeper concepts that lead to understanding. What is learned must go beyond material with "right" answers; it must be connected across subjects and with the real world.

Boyer's concept of learning displays some contradictions; but it is clear that he believes that learning should be an active, involving process. He argues for a new requirement that all students engage in an extensive community service project; it and much other learning must occur outside classrooms and off campus. Yet, in a discussion of the diminishing ability of vocational education to prepare students for an increasing diversity of jobs, he fails to consider the notion of moving such training into the workplace.

Lightfoot's students look to teachers for guidance in their learning. The best students are dedicated, inquiring individuals who display enough dependence to make their teachers feel comfortable, important, and needed; but in groups they are a force with which to be reckoned. Good teachers in her "good" high schools display "fearlessness"; they are "unafraid of these young people who tend to baffle and offend the rest of us" (p. 343).

Boyer, too, raises the issue of fear. He quotes a principal:

> Adults drive past our high school quickly. Sometimes they avoid
> it entirely, particularly if they see groups of teenagers hanging

around outside. I think they're illustrating something I've lately come to believe — that there's a fear of adolescents in this country. Few adults understand them, and most find them hard to like. What we do feel is that they must be controlled. (p. 205)

Many, the Commission included, probably would interpret this fearfulness that even good high schools have as a further sign of the serious erosion of a once useful institution. This says much about the abysmal conditions under which we expect learning and teaching to occur. Have we lost sight so completely of what constitutes a reasonable situation in which to *require* people's presence? By what criterion can we term a high school *good,* as Lightfoot does, that requires good teachers to be fearless? For us, it is a measure of the degree to which the high school has been unable to adapt to dramatic changes in adolescents. Adolescents have become, in a sense, unmanageable in large numbers. What was the high school's forte two generations ago — mass education — has become its Achilles' heel.

The Commission's view of students and learning stands in stark contrast to the other four presentations. Because it is a much shorter treatise than the others, comparing its treatment of students and learning to the others is somewhat unfair. But the punitive tone in *A Nation at Risk* is clear. Students have been allowed to become laggards and must now be shaped up. Schools must get down to the *business* of learning. Students must be required to do more homework and to attend school more days. Learning occurs in a typical, segmented curriculum. *A Nation at Risk* does not discuss learning as a personal act. Rather, learning is what students are required to do for the sake of the nation; and students should be held accountable, through increased testing, for meeting that expectation. Students are exhorted to take hold of their lives and work with dedication (even if what they are asked to do has little immediate meaning for them).

Our own view is that the typical contemporary American high school is much more effective as an instrument for controlling and confining adolescents than as a means for teaching them. Very little of the high school experience is congruent with the findings of learning research or of common sense. Several of these authors describe the fragmentation of knowledge, the emphasis on coverage at the expense of the establishment of personal meaning, the tyranny of a time schedule that precludes lengthy discourse or introspection, and a concept of mass education that emasculates attempts to individualize learning.

The way we keep school — in other words, its culture — must change significantly. We have chosen to deal with students in groups so large that the resentment and cynicism they spawn overwhelm the attempts that teachers make to personalize the high school experience. Should it surprise us that youths, in growing numbers, are not "buying" high school anymore? Should it surprise us that so many reject it and whatever opportunities for learning it does offer?

Teachers and the Act of Teaching

Lightfoot, Goodlad, and Sizer all describe the isolation teachers feel, and how little time teachers have to collaborate or even collectively deliberate. Boyer also points out the degree to which teachers are outside the governance pattern of the school and describes the problems caused by bureaucratic constraints under which teachers may be told not only what textbook to use but, in some cases, how to use it. Lightfoot also sees the disparity of power between teachers and administrators in some schools, where teachers "are sometimes made to feel like children" (p. 339).

Such constraints lead Goodlad to view teaching as a trade rather than a profession. Sizer reinforces this view:

> Teachers are told the amount of time they are to spend with each class — say, fifty-five minutes five times a week. Even though they are expected to be competent scholars, they are rarely trusted with the selection of the texts and teaching materials they are to use, a particularly galling insult. Teachers are rarely consulted, much less given significant authority, over the rules and regulations governing the life of their school; these usually come from "downtown." Rarely do they have any influence over who their immediate colleagues will be; again, "downtown" decides. One wonders how good a law firm would be if it were given manuals on how to apply the law, were told precisely how much time to spend on each case, were directed how to govern its internal affairs, and had no say whatever in who the partners were. Teaching often lacks a sense of ownership, a sense among the teachers working together that the school is theirs, and that its future and their reputation are indistinguishable. Hired hands own nothing, are told what to do, and have little stake in their enterprises. Teachers are often treated like hired hands. Not surprisingly, they often act like hired hands. (p. 184)

Teaching is a highly underrated act, an observation with which all these authors would no doubt agree. Good teaching requires good judgment. For Sizer, the teacher is one of three factors — the others being the student and the content — that must be balanced and rebalanced, a highly complex act. Goodlad describes a dyad, teaching and the cir-

11

cumstances of schooling; for him, everything depends on the interaction between these two factors.

For Sizer, good teaching is a form of theater, a position with which Lightfoot would likely agree. Many of her descriptions of good teaching take on theatrical qualities: charismatic "stars," "grande dames," and "mensches" who thrive in the existing high school environment (p. 342). Sizer argues strongly for teaching as a form of coaching, the act of assessing each student's performance in order to improve it. Coaching would replace much of the telling, the teaching approach that now dominates classrooms.

The Commission also sees the conditions under which teaching occurs to have eroded badly. While it does not discuss the act of teaching, one may deduce that the Commission's good teacher is a demanding taskmaster, a no-nonsense, goal-oriented individual. Many teachers are seen as sub-par, without talent, aimless, perhaps even lazy. These teachers must shape up by meeting higher standards determined by competency testing. Significantly higher salaries, a longer teaching year, and a career ladder culminating in master teacher status are key elements of the Commission's plan for making teaching once again attractive to a wider, more talented segment of college graduates.

Our own view is that the needs of teachers and the demands of teaching are key criteria for reforming the high school. High schools have not worked well for students for some time. The reason for the current perception of a crisis is that the high school no longer works for teachers. Many teachers have simply left teaching. Many more have psychologically withdrawn; they have surrendered to unworkable circumstances in sufficient numbers to arouse the entire nation.

Good teaching requires that reasonable limits be placed on the complexity of the situation in which we expect the act to be performed; it requires few enough students for the individual learning problems of each to be diagnosed and addressed. It requires time: time to think about what is most important to teach, time to discuss important issues with colleagues, and time to recharge ones psychic batteries before the next class.

We do not disagree that it would be good for the high school to establish incentives to attract more exceptional teachers. But Goodlad is likely right when he implies that those now teaching probably have had better training than current conditions permit them to use. Only after establishing conditions in which well-meaning, right-thinking individuals — mere mortals rather than Superteachers — can put forth a reasonable effort and be successful can we begin to identify the marginally competent and the truly lazy within the profession.

Governance and Students, Teachers, and Parents

Youth have changed in many ways, yet they continue to be processed through the fundamentally unchanged institution of the high school. Because of medical and nutritional advances, each generation of adolescents has physically matured earlier than its predecessor; each is physically larger than its predecessor. The automobile and the youth-oriented market offer many illusions of adulthood to the young. All of these factors tell adolescents that they are important, that their wishes are legitimate, and that their desires are attainable. The high school itself has contributed to this change by segregating large masses of adolescents from the adult world for significant lengths of time; the high school is the Petri dish in which the youth culture has grown.

On the other hand, in high school they are expected, as their grandparents were, to do what they are told. In high school they are told what they should consider important. In high school their time is mostly governed by someone else. In high school many of them are told, in many subtle ways, that they are insignificant. These messages, as Sizer points out, are increasingly rejected:

> Their apparent acquiescence to what their elders want them to do is always provisional. . . . [A] challenge can be made by students in any classroom when, for whatever reason, they collectively, quietly, but assuredly decide to say no. The fact that most go along with the system masks the nascent power that students hold. Few adults outside the teaching profession understand this. (p. 140)

These five books say very little about the role of students, teachers, and parents in the governance of high schools. Lightfoot does relate an incident in which two girls in a large high school try to influence their principal to hire a particular teacher. He listens to their case and will look into it. Their suggestions are not a normal part of the hiring process; they are the politely received pleadings of the disenfranchised, not the necessary input of an important segment of the school community.

Boyer displays a concern about the degree to which adolescents are told what to do in high school. After describing several classroom situations, he laments,

> These vignettes of the American classroom raise disturbing questions about how instruction relates to the professed goals of edu-

13

cation. How, for example, can the relatively passive and docile roles of students prepare them to participate as informed, active, and questioning citizens? How can the regimented schedule and the routinized atmosphere of classrooms prepare students for independence as adults? Not least, how can we produce critical and creative thinking throughout a student's life when we so systematically discourage individuality in the classroom? (p. 147)

Note that this is not a governance issue for Boyer; rather, it is an instructional one. Yet, this is as close as he gets to a discussion of student, teacher, or parental involvement in the governance of the high school.

Goodlad sees a wider role for adolescents in setting the direction of the high school:

> They are not too immature, too inexperienced, or too innocent for the tasks involved. Many of them have conceived babies, many drink alcohol and take drugs, some hold jobs, all will be eligible to vote soon. Our young people get caught up in the values, problems, and vices of adulthood at an early age. They are delayed unduly in assuming authority and responsibility commensurate with this early orientation to adult society. Why not call on them now to join with adults in tackling the problems of youth in and out of schools — the problems which, clearly, adults are failing to solve by themselves? I think our youth is ready to respond. (p. 88)

Goodlad has little to say about the teacher's or parent's role. That teachers are key actors in tailoring his proposed nationally designed curricula to the needs of their students and communities is clear, but their part in *governing* the school is not discussed. Do they have no role?

The Commission makes no mention of governance, but much of the Commission's rhetoric imposes standards on the performance of teachers and students and firm limits on their autonomy.

Sizer disagrees directly with the Commission on the standards issue. In a contrived conversation with a hypothetical, somewhat skeptical principal, the principal asks,

> *What of standards?*
>
> The existence of final "exhibitions" by students as a condition to receiving their diplomas will give teachers a much greater control of standards than they currently have. These standards, combined with a variety of external examinations, such as the Advanced Placement Examination of the College Board, Regents' Examinations in some states, and it is hoped, a growing list of other

instruments that a school or an individual student could adopt or take voluntarily, would give outside authorities, like regional accrediting agencies, a good sense of the quality of work being done.

A lot turns on those teachers. Are they good enough?

They've got to be. (p. 138, emphasis in original)

Governance of a school entails far more than the single responsibility of setting standards. It apparently is an important issue for Sizer; for example, he observes how much more control teachers in private schools have in setting their school's direction and, perhaps as a result, how much less disillusioned they are.

In our view, governance is a critical issue. The degree to which students, parents, and even teachers are excluded from a role in establishing their school's direction and standards is a part of the problem. That these five books, several of which rely heavily on teacher and student interview data, can ignore the issue dismays us. Are these authors' respondents not raising the issue? We know from our own research work that if one *asks* teachers and students in a large high school about governance, they express concern, even anger, in describing their lack of involvement. Are these authors' perspectives so restricted that alternative governance models are not even considered?

Program

Four of these books describe at some length their ideal program of study for the high school (Lightfoot's chosen role is that of reporter rather than reformer). To varying degrees, these four books call for a common curriculum that *all* students not only experience, but achieve.

Boyer's curriculum is built on achieving four essential goals:

> First, the high school should help all students develop the capacity to think critically and communicate effectively through a mastery of language.
> Second, the high school should help all students learn about themselves, the human heritage, and the interdependent world in which they live through a core curriculum based upon consequential human experiences common to all people.
> Third, the high school should prepare all students for work and further education through a program of electives that develop individual aptitudes and interests.
> Fourth, the high school should help all students fulfill their social and civic obligations through school and community service. (pp. 66-67)

15

To accomplish these ends, Boyer proposes a core curriculum that dominates the first two years of high school with electives and a community-service requirement in the final two years. Boyer terms these final two years the transition school, which purposefully prepares students for life after high school. Boyer's common curriculum includes mastering the skills of reading, writing, speaking, listening, and computing. A sound program for him, however, must move beyond simply acquiring essential skills to achieving cultural literacy. Literature, the arts, foreign languages, history of the United States and Western civilizations, and non-Western studies would all contribute to a fundamental cultural requirement. The required curriculum also would include civics, science, mathematics, technology, health, a seminar on work, and an independent project during the senior year. While Boyer describes each of these as separate entities, he stresses that they should not be taught that way. Each discipline's current state of "splendid isolation" must be replaced by "a new interdisciplinary vision" (pp. 114-15). Boyer stresses that electives, too, must be purposeful. They should constitute a connected program, carefully planned for each student. Boyer would replace the SAT, which he terms "the most dramatic rite of passage for many students" (p. 132), with a more universally applicable Student Achievement and Advisement Test that would be an appropriate measure of the achievement of all students, not just the college-bound.

The Commission also calls for a national curriculum built around what it terms the "Five New Basics": English, mathematics, science, social studies, and computer science. What is "new" about four of these five is not clear. Foreign languages and the arts are important, but clearly less so than these basics. That computer science can have so quickly surpassed curriculum mainstays like foreign languages and the arts is consistent with what we can best term the corporate undertone of the Commission's report; if the business of America is business, the business of high school is getting students ready for business. The Commission, like Boyer, would ensure an emphasis on its five basics through a stringent assessment program.

Goodlad describes a 10-year program, required of all students, that would coincide with the existing limits of compulsory schooling. A mastery learning approach would replace simply putting in time in the common school. Equality of access to knowledge is a key; Goodlad, like all these authors, decries tracking. Through improved teaching techniques combined with the more efficient use of instructional time, Goodlad speculates that students would achieve an equal or superior

16

program to the current 12-year curriculum. Some would be ready to enter college directly upon completion of this program; others might continue their studies in community colleges or vocational programs.

Goodlad favors state guidelines rather than requirements as criteria for designing a balanced program for all students. Such a program contains "the 'five fingers' of human knowledge and organized experience — mathematics and science, literature and language, society and social studies, the arts, [and] the vocations" (p. 286). High schools now provide this program, but the "degree of school-to-school variability" that currently exists must not be allowed (p. 287). How we teach (covering topics, using set materials and quizzes), not what we teach, is the problem. Schools must teach common concepts, principles, and skills — not topics. Individual differences require teaching common content in different ways. Curriculum building would occur in national development centers rather than at the local level.

All of these authors presume the state's right to make, as Sizer puts it, "claims on the minds and actions of its citizens" (p. 86). This tenet is basic to compulsory school attendance. Sizer argues that the state often oversteps its bounds; its requirements should be confined to literacy, numeracy, and civic understanding. Sharing Goodlad's concern about the potential excesses of a national curriculum, Sizer stresses the need to tailor curricula to:

> the conditions peculiar to each school. Master plans for cities, states, and the nation that standardize instruction are certain to be inefficient; no one set of procedures can conceivably serve most students well. (p. 115)

Sizer's minimal goals for the high school are summarized in three questions:

> Can graduates of this high school teach themselves? Are they decent people? Can they effectively use the principal ways of looking at the world, ways represented by the major and traditional academic disciplines? (p. 131)

To accomplish these goals and minimize the fragmentation of knowledge into subjects that now characterizes the high school, Sizer would organize the high school and its curriculum around four areas: Inquiry and Expression, Mathematics and Science, Literature and the Arts, and Philosophy and History (p. 132).

Our view is that those goals of schooling that would make each of us a responsible social animal and those that would make each of us a uniquely capable, fully functioning human being are inherently con-

17

tradictory. Any curriculum is flawed that does not sort these two tasks
— socialization and developing the creative intellect. A good curriculum must make the differences between these tasks evident to teachers, parents, and students; and it must develop measures for accomplishing both. The fundamental skills that one needs to function as a useful member of society must be acquired; but a program that stops there, that does not capitalize on the strengths of each individual, is incomplete. It cheats students of a reasonable opportunity to become the individuals they are capable of becoming. If they are lucky or privileged enough, the circumstances of their lives will compensate for the deficiency; they will become capable human beings despite the high school. Such a program also cheats society by depriving it of the rich variability that it needs to adapt to changing conditions. In Chapter 6 we will describe in considerable detail a high school that attends to these two contradictory sets of needs.

The Blind Spot Toward Structure

A change in the *structure* of the high school is of critical importance to reform, but these five books are handicapped by ignoring structure. Only Lightfoot and Sizer look at schools without standard structures. Lightfoot's exceptions were elite private academies and the small school-within-a-school that by happenstance existed in one of her large suburban high schools. Sizer claims to have visited many unconventional high schools. In describing the tensions that develop in pluralistic communities he concedes:

> Inevitably, some communities will be too split to accommodate
> their values in one school, to reconcile their differing specific defini-
> tions of decent conduct. However, there can be as much refresh-
> ing strength in the tension over values as there are seeds for discord.
> Many communities handle this tension by giving families choices,
> with a "traditional" program or an "alternative" (for which read
> "liberal") program within the public system or with private schools.
> Many of these options are formally identified primarily as academic
> alternatives, rather than one of a value-laden ethos. My hunch, af-
> ter seeing many, is that it is their tone — the people in them and
> the way that values affect their *structure* — that gives them their
> appeal. These are, in fact, options for different sorts of character
> education. Within legal and commonsensical limits, such options
> should be available to all families. (p. 130, emphasis added)

The handicap of ignoring the structure of schools is most vivid in the juxtaposition of the problems these authors perceive and their proposed solutions. For example, many of Boyer's recommendations are inadequate in light of his own analysis of the severity of the problems faced by the high school. Boyer lists some of these problems:

> The threat of physical violence in the schools has received considerable attention. The problem is, in fact, very real. Teachers in some schools do not feel safe in the halls, in the parking lots, or even in the classrooms. A recent *New York Times* poll of over five thousand randomly selected teachers revealed that one-third of New York City teachers and one-fourth of those elsewhere said they had been assaulted. Forty percent reported that violence is a daily concern. . . .
>
> In 1981, more than one-third (36 percent) of the high school teachers said they would not or "probably" would not go into teaching if they had it to do over again. This is almost twice as many (19 percent) as felt that way in 1976, and almost three times as many (13 percent) as felt that way in 1971. . . .
>
> In sum, the teacher's world is often frustrating, frequently demeaning, and sometimes dangerous. The result for many teachers is a sense of alienation, apathy, and what is now fashionably called "teacher burnout." (p. 159)

Boyer *immediately* goes on to list remedies, presumably to these problems: Limit teachers' loads to "four formal class meetings." Teachers should have "a minimum of sixty minutes each school day for class preparation." They "should be exempt from routine monitoring of halls and lunch rooms." And "the intellectual climate of the school" should be improved (pp. 159-60).

What any of these remedies has to do with teacher assaults is difficult to ascertain. Perhaps by reducing teachers' class loads and other contacts with students, the percentage of assaults will drop accordingly. Boyer does not seem to see that these problems are symptomatic of an institution that no longer functions effectively. These recommendations tinker with some of the symptoms, but they ignore the central problem. Boyer's primary recourse is to blame the problem on people: students and teachers have changed and no longer fit the high school; therefore they, not the concept of the high school itself, must change.

In a similar manner, Goodlad builds a case for the importance of teacher satisfaction and describes the "more satisfying" schools in his sample. Understandably, they have fewer and less intense problems than "less satisfying" schools. Goodlad continues his analysis:

> Disturbingly, 10 of the 14 "less satisfying" schools in our sample served primarily black, Mexican-American, or racially mixed student populations. Of the 10 "more satisfying" schools selected from all levels, only two served such populations; the other eight enrolled predominantly white students. We must note that some of

these "more satisfying" schools were small and that *the relationship between small schools and teacher satisfaction just mentioned was substantial.* Nonetheless, the data suggest teachers encounter some added difficulties affecting their satisfaction in schools serving nearly all minority or mixed student populations. (p. 180, emphasis added)

Goodlad seems to view school size as the important factor in these results. In raising the issue of size, Goodlad has made the beginnings of a case for the consideration of new structural models for schooling, as he does at numerous points in the book. And he argues effectively that the problem is more than simply a people problem, that the structure no longer works. Yet he deflects his recommendation for new structures to other agencies *outside* the school.

The school alone cannot handle problems once shared and controlled by home, church, and school working hand-in-hand. If these earlier collaborations cannot be rebuilt, then perhaps *we need new configurations of agencies and institutions* sensitive to changing circumstances. (p. 74, emphasis added)

Goodlad has a structural blind spot. He does not consider new forms of schooling, even after presenting considerable data in support of such a move. After convincing us that people are not the central problem, he optimistically concludes that we are well on our way to solving the problem of schooling — by changing people:

A reality of recent years is that our schools — particularly high schools — have been absorbing increasingly diverse student populations. This trend will continue. Principals and teachers have been strained in seeking to cope with problems they probably were not well equipped to handle.

It is likely, however, that the greatest strains are now of the past. Educators are learning more about these circumstances and how to deal with them. Special preparation is now a part of many teacher education programs. Whereas desegregation and integration have been the central goals, providing quality education for all students is now paramount. Let us hope that equity and quality can be achieved simultaneously. This is a challenge, of course, that cannot be met successfully by teachers alone. (p. 182)

Over and over, Goodlad approaches a call for structural change in schools, and over and over he avoids completing the argument. Are new forms of schooling so unimaginable? It appears more likely that Goodlad simply sees them as a politically unrealistic and, therefore, a pragmatically bankrupt alternative. Or, perhaps, he simply cannot envision a markedly different structure that still offers a comprehensive curriculum.

Lightfoot's portrayal of six high schools does not include the sort of explicit recommendations that we are using here to reveal structural blind spots. She gives high schools the benefit of the doubt, perhaps to a fault. Lightfoot is a portrait painter, not a reformer. Only after reading almost the entire book do we encounter what we infer to be her position on the structure of the high school.

> The search for "good" schools is elusive and disappointing if by goodness we mean something close to perfection. These portraits of good schools reveal imperfections, uncertainties, and vulnerabilities in each of them. In fact, one could argue that a consciousness about imperfections, and the willingness to admit them and search for their origins and solutions is one of the important ingredients of goodness in schools. (p. 309)

We take this concept to mean that the good high school is one in which the people working in it have managed to be relatively effective despite the handicaps its structure places on them. But as an institution becomes increasingly out-of-sync with its evolving social context, should we be satisfied with its being increasingly ineffective? Lightfoot offers no counsel on the point at which one breaks free of the deepening quagmire.

We believe that the high school will not improve significantly until we dramatically alter its current structure. That requires fundamentally transforming the high school culture, with which its structure constantly interacts. High schools must be reduced in size to the point where control is no longer their prime concern. Teachers and students must be given a major role in setting each school's course; and these small schools must be allowed to develop differently, not only from the typical high school, but from one another.

Community

One need look no further than the title of this book to realize that we place great importance on the sense of community in a high school. In some ways, the concept is a composite of all the factors discussed in this chapter; we believe it is the critical concept. Without a sense of community that includes both students and teachers, keeping school becomes a continuous, uphill struggle requiring the expenditure of considerable professional energies just to stop bad things from happening.

This view apparently is not shared by the majority of the authors discussed in this chapter. Sizer says nothing about community directly; his careful analysis and description of the individual human condition seldom extends to the collective. None of his recommendations touches directly on the issue of improving community.

In an otherwise very thorough analysis, Goodlad, too, ignores community. The high school's need to meet the personal goals of students receives extensive attention. The ambiance of a school is discussed, but not its sense of community. Nowhere does Goodlad mention the concept as we use it here.

There is no place for such concerns in the Commission's task- and achievement-oriented high school. It is probable that teachers and students would be encouraged to compete rather than cooperate under the pressures the Commission would impose. The Commission's position is not clear on the issue, but the following line of reasoning carries little risk of being unfair: achievement leads to higher levels of self-esteem and peer acceptance; self-esteem and peer acceptance lead to easier, more cordial relationships with others, which in turn lead to an improved sense of community. The model is designed for winners at the expense of losers. It is, in other words, a call for business as usual with regard to the social climate of the high school.

Boyer does not ignore community, but we are not certain he understands it. One of the successful high schools he studied had as a goal, "build a spirit of community and service" (p. 66). However, Boyer alters this in an important respect when he attempts to explain it. The phrase "spirit of community" is replaced; the goal becomes, "the high school should help all students fulfill their social and civic obligations through school and community service" (p. 67).

Boyer discusses the importance of a shared vision and embraces Dewey's concept of groups "working along common lines, in a common spirit, and with reference to common aims" (p. 215), but it always gets translated into his laudable idea of a community-service requirement. For Boyer, these ideas are important to maintaining and improving the larger social fabric. High schools prepare students to experience community and instill in students the values and skills to improve community, but high schools apparently do not need to model these virtues.

Lightfoot gives some attention to community and comes closest of these authors in sharing our concern about its importance. She notes the demise of "school spirit, the sense of belonging that students felt in the sixties" that capably substituted for a sense of community in the large high schools of that era.

> "Sports events no longer bring people together as they still do in some less affluent communities." Kline [a head counselor] describes the deterioration of a sense of community within the school and says many students feel isolated and alone as they move through their day. Highland Park [one of Lightfoot's suburban settings] has become an "exclusionary community . . . the tone of the school dominated by a superficial sophistication . . . the primary preoccupations are in finding the right clothes, the right kind of car, the right friends." The troubles inside the school reflect a "depressive core in the community," worries Kline. Without goals or traditions to unite energies, hostility is directed inward and divisions intensify. "The Italians are offended by the loose affluence of the Jewish kids," and the students from the army base seem "rigid, uptight, and conservative." Differences are exaggerated. (p. 137)

Lightfoot also understands how size impedes community. "People are more likely to feel a sense of community in small institutions. The scale is important to members' feelings of belonging, visibility, and effectiveness" (p. 346).

In our view any reasonable sense of community has been lost in the typical American high school. Outmoded models of leadership and practices like tracking have pitted segments of the student population against one another. Competition has been an overused motivational device. Cooperation and mutual support have languished as participants in larger and larger institutions segregate themselves into tighter and tighter cliques. The high school must change, or it will be replaced by institutions more in step with the needs of today's students and teachers. Building a sense of community is the most fundamental step in that rebuilding process, but it is an extremely difficult task in the large high schools we have created.

This book attempts to describe how educators can begin that rebuilding process. We wish to make one optimistic point: The change will not be easy, but we already know most of what we need to know. Working models exist of public high schools that have successfully made the transition. Emulating these existing schools represents the high school's best hope of once again becoming a viable social institution.

Chapter 2
Two Schools — Two Cultures

Schools began with a man under a tree, a man who did not know he was a teacher, discussing his realizations with a few others who did not know they were students. The students reflected on the exchanges between them and on how good it was to be in the presence of this man. They wished their sons, also, to listen to such a man. Soon, the needed spaces were erected and the first schools came into existence. The establishment of schools was inevitable because they are part of the desires of man. Our vast systems of education, now vested in institutions, stem from these little schools, but the spirit of their beginning is now forgotten.

—Louis I. Kahn

The influence that school size and culture wield can be demonstrated by describing two high schools in a single community.* Both are subject to the same policies, standards, and expectations of their commu-

---

*In May 1982 we spent one week collecting data, observing, and interviewing participants in these two schools. Additional data were collected the previous year. Quantitative data — our *Statements About School Inventory* (Smith, Gregory, and Pugh 1981) — were collected from 446 students and 124 teachers in two separate testings a year apart. Individual or small-group interviews were conducted with 54 students and 24 teachers and administrators in the two schools. This research was supported, in part, by the Maris-Proffit Endowment of the Indiana University School of Education.

24

nity. Both are funded in the same way. Yet they have become two very different high schools.

One is a typical high school — we will call it "Gulliver High School." Despite our label, with one thousand students and about 70 teachers it is small by comprehensive high school standards. In our judgment, it is a fine example of its type. It reflects the high academic standards of its teachers and the university community in which it resides. Many of its teachers and, we suspect, the community in general view it as one of the best high schools in the state. Most neutral observers probably would agree. Its faculty is well trained in the academic subjects, and its progressive administrators set high expectations. Its curriculum is like that of most high schools, offering a breadth of courses including advanced levels in several subjects. English, social studies, the sciences, mathematics, and foreign languages constitute the "basics." Its programs in art, music, and sports receive statewide attention.

The second high school — we will call it "Lilliput High School" — is housed in a portion of an elementary school. It is small, with about 175 students and about 12 faculty. It has no varsity sports, no large musical performance groups, and a much more limited range of formal course offerings.

Our naming of these two schools may, at first, seem flippant. It is really quite considered. The larger high school, like Gulliver of Swift's *Gulliver's Travels,* seemed quite normal until we viewed it in the context of a markedly different scale. Just as Gulliver began to look odd in his new context, the practices of this normal, everyday high school began to look strange to us as we experienced them alongside those of its smaller sister school.

Size is not the only difference between these schools, for Lilliput has consciously chosen to embrace a quite different philosophy, curriculum, and governance structure. Hundreds, perhaps thousands, of public high schools satisfy the descriptor of "small," but only a few dozen have taken the important next step and have consciously worked to develop a cohesive school culture. Most of these small public high schools are alternative schools. Some prefer to term them "public schools of choice," in part because *alternative* was first identified with the private free-school movement of the late 1960s, and in part because the term *alternative* has been applied more recently to the dumping grounds that many school systems and even entire states have created for "problem students." The small school described here is a purposefully different form of education, freely available to every student in the community. Its heterogeneous student body reflects that policy.

Our original intent in studying these two schools was to assess similarities and differences in their social climates. Indeed, we found large and intriguing differences, not only in their climates but in many other areas. We came to realize how different from one another schools can be, even schools in the same small town. The monolithic structure that has characterized the American high school for generations is a familiar model. Other models exist; but because they are relatively new, they are suspect. A central point of our argument is that because they are new, they fit today's students and teachers better than does the model conceived for their grandparents.

The Sense of Community

Broadly speaking, American education may be thought of as trying to respond to two basic and, in some ways, conflicting values. One of these, individuality, leads a school to strive to enhance the unique talents, interests, and skills of each student. The other, community, leads a school to strive to develop the sense that each person belongs to a group and feels some commitment to it, that each is responsible to the others for his or her actions. Both these schools tend to place more emphasis on individuality — though each interprets the concept somewhat differently — than on community. However, Lilliput's students and teachers speak more frequently and intensely about community than do their counterparts at Gulliver.

One of the common themes in interviews conducted at Lilliput was the understanding and acceptance of diversity. Individuals can be different and yet still get along and appreciate the uniqueness of others. This sentiment contrasted sharply with the cliquishness that exists at Gulliver. There, each group tends to accept only a relatively narrow range of differences and speaks in negative terms about other groups in the school. One female student at Lilliput expresses it this way:

> There is a tendency to group there [at Gulliver] because there are
> so many people that you feel the need to belong with somebody
> all the time. At [Lilliput] you can be your own person and meet
> people as people and not as a group.

Despite Gulliver's cliques, its students often emphasized individuality as a major theme. As one student said, "I came from the northeastern part of the state and there was unity [within] the school. I mean the classes worked together. Here, I think individuality is stressed more than the group." Another Gulliver student stated, "Everybody's in their own group of friends and there's no mass attitude. Like everyone's either for yourself or yourself and a few other people." To put it another way, diversity at Lilliput seems based on a respect for individual differences, whereas diversity at Gulliver seems to exist between groups that are generally antagonistic toward each other.

There is a stronger sense of community at Lilliput. To begin with, teachers and students share a fairly harmonious set of values. A much broader set of values exists at Gulliver, and the differences among these values often are difficult to reconcile; as a result, there is little foundation on which to build unity. The stronger sense of community at Lilliput is manifested in knowing each other's names, calling teachers by their first names, open-ended friendship groups (rather than closed cliques), and a sense of responsibility to the school as a community. Comments from two students express these qualities quite clearly:

> I certainly feel like it's [Lilliput] more of a family than any other school that I've gone to.

> Yeah, but it's [the sense of community] much more than I've ever felt at any other school.

A number of teachers at Gulliver experience a sense of isolation. While they make an effort to get acquainted with individual students, they apparently do not make the same effort to know each other. One teacher, who had been in the school for five years, received a telephone call from another teacher asking her out on a date. Because she could not place a face with his name, she had to ask around to identify him before accepting the invitation.

Gulliver's teachers tend to interact within departmental groups, in part because the architecture of the school reinforces such associations. In contrasting Gulliver with another school — not Lilliput — a teacher spoke of the "individuality of teachers" at Gulliver and concluded that "teachers tend to be less team-oriented." Another described the low levels of interaction, and a third spoke about "a lack of a sense of community in terms of faculty working together." It is not so much that faculty are split into two or more camps that are at odds with one another as it is that they tend to go their own ways. Only one of the 14 teachers we interviewed at Gulliver said he enjoyed "the esprit de corps" or made any similar reference.

Both students and teachers acknowledge at Gulliver the value of a sense of community, and both groups are aware that the administration is making an effort to do something about the problem. As one teacher said, "I know [that] one of the goals of the present administration is to try to create a sense of community among all students, faculty, and administration — everybody." Another teacher put it this way: "I think they're [the administrators] trying to mold . . . some kind of feeling for the school. They're trying to have the students have some kind of feeling that this is their school." That this teacher viewed community as an important goal for students but did not mention it as a need or goal for teachers may be symptomatic of the low expectations for community we sensed among Gulliver's faculty.

Teachers and Students

Because of differences in size and educational philosophy, the teachers and students in both high schools behave quite differently with their peers and members of the other group. Regarding teachers, we have concluded that we were observing two quite different definitions of professionalism. The teachers at Gulliver believe in maintaining a certain amount of social distance between themselves and their students. They are open and friendly with students and speak to them casually about a great many matters, but they take care not to go "too far" in becoming "chummy" with students. Their role as teachers requires them to evaluate and pass judgment; becoming too close to students makes this task difficult to do with objectivity.

Lilliput's teachers take a different tack, viewing themselves not so much as teachers as resident adults, persons to whom students can turn if they have academic or personal problems. They try to break down the separation between students' and teachers' roles. Indeed, some classes are taught by students; teachers may sit in on them as much to learn as to teach. Teachers breach the wall of separation by permitting students to call them by their first names, by dressing in clothes not that much different from typical student garb, and by not setting aside private space (such as a teachers' lounge) that is not accessible to students. Like a family, all members of the community live in and share a communal space. Lilliput's size makes this arrangement workable. The easy, casual atmosphere that pervades the school is not something from which teachers feel a need to escape.

Lilliput's teachers go beyond these relatively superficial ways of eliminating what they consider to be the artificial roles of student and teacher. Informal activities, such as picnics, field trips, and overnights — where such roles hold little utility — occur frequently. Some teachers take this a step further, inviting students to their homes or going to movies or other activities with them. Whereas Gulliver's teachers deliberately maintain the separation between student and teacher, Lilliput's faculty work to eliminate it.

Structures

These two schools differ markedly in the way in which they conceptualize the space, time, content, and governance structures that affect their day-to-day experiences. Both students and teachers at Gulliver seem to be tightly bound by existing structures. They are givens not to be tampered with and tolerated in order to get the job done.

At Lilliput, givens are more likely to be viewed as something that can and will be changed if the need arises. Teachers encourage students to take an active role in framing what they will study, how they will study it, and how they will evaluate it. While Lilliput adheres to the same state requirements and school board policies as Gulliver, it does not seem as bound to the standard curriculum. In this regard, teachers exercise considerable power over their professional lives.

Gulliver's teachers generally think of the classroom as the crucible of learning, the place where it all happens. If pressed, many would probably agree that learning can take place in other settings; but they do not embrace the concept seriously enough to make it work. Such changes are difficult in large institutions; there are more important battles to be waged. As a consequence, Gulliver's teachers are as bolted to their classrooms as were desks in an earlier era.

At Gulliver, time rules all. For the teacher, there often is too little time; for the student, there often is too much. Teachers can never cover all the material they need to; and many students, some of whom have as many as four study halls a day, speak of boredom. One innovation being implemented at Gulliver during our visit was an extra period two days each week for teachers to work with students on a more informal basis. Most teachers opposed the change because they lost six minutes from every other period. They needed those six minutes to "cover the material."

At Gulliver the prescribed curriculum must be covered in the daily allotment of time; there is little time for exploring topics of interest. Such restrictions hamper the creative teacher and encourage students to assume only minimal responsibility for what they learn. Thus students and, to a lesser degree, teachers feel little sense of accountability for what is learned or taught; that is someone else's requirement.

29

At Lilliput, time seems less a tyrant to be obeyed than a resource to be exploited. Lilliput's informal approach makes it relatively easy to tie subject matter to students' lives. While subject matter does have intrinsic worth, its chief value is for teaching more universal skills. Lilliput's teachers are less likely to follow assiduously a prescribed curriculum. The school's structure enables them more easily to make adjustments for the reading level of the student and for the interests and talents of both students and teachers. The textbook is less likely to represent the primary source of information. A wider variety of materials with differing points of view, some chosen by the students themselves, is likely to be employed. Indeed, the standard textbook approach was largely absent in the classes we observed. In general, Lilliput's teachers exercise considerable autonomy in selecting materials. Gulliver's teachers probably have a similar autonomy, but the nature of the institution in which they work seems to discourage such initiatives.

Governance

Size greatly determines governance practices. The town meeting, which continues to work well in a New Hampshire hamlet, is a ludicrous format in Boston. The larger the high school, the more difficult the task of enfranchising students and even teachers. Size as a factor in governance is readily apparent in these two schools.

Gulliver's governance structures tend to exclude students and even teachers from important decisions about the life of the school, thus creating a we/they attitude between students and teachers. Consequently, students tend to resist what they consider to be an imposed set of rules, regulations, and policies that govern their behavior. Since they have little role in constructing the structures that govern them, they feel little obligation to conform to them. Being told to behave as adults without being trusted to do so leads students to engage in intricate games of subterfuge that clearly display their disrespect for the system but fall short of requiring serious reprimand.

Gulliver does have a typical student council, which gives a few students a role in advising the principal on matters of student concern. In contrast, Lilliput's governance structure is the town-meeting format. These all-school meetings operate on the principle of one person, one vote. Students and teachers debate issues as equals. Implicit in the system is the presumption that students will act maturely and responsibly and will not misuse the power their overwhelming majority gives them. They apparently do not. There is a check mechanism: the principal can veto any decision that students and teachers make if, in his judgment, it endangers the school's existence. He has never had to exercise it.

Student and teacher involvement in the governance of Lilliput goes further. The lifeblood of any school is its faculty. Hiring good teachers is probably the most important set of decisions any school can make. In large schools, interviewing and hiring is usually the exclusive responsibility of the principal and other building administrators. As size increases, even the principal may relinquish this duty to the central administration. At Lilliput each vacancy is filled by a hiring committee comprised of several students and teachers and the principal. No prospective teacher that the students did not want has ever been offered a position.

Most people, students and teachers included, want to feel that they are responsible agents of their institutions and are not there simply to do someone else's bidding. DeCharms (1976) makes the distinction between what he terms origins and pawns. Origins are in control of their lives; they make things happen; they take responsibility for their acts; they are powerful in a positive way. Pawns have no sense of being in control; they are controlled by others; they have no internal compass providing direction. Pawns (from the Old French *peon* meaning foot soldier) are expendable; they have little intrinsic value.

At Gulliver, most students and even some teachers perceive themselves as pawns. Virtually all students with whom we spoke felt they were more or less under the control of others. They are told what to do and when to do it. In the case of teachers, the issue is professional autonomy; for example, many teachers see the principal as manipulative and authoritarian. One teacher described a petition that accused the principal of usurping teachers' responsibilities as professionals. Those circulating that petition most certainly were pawns aspiring to be origins.

In many ways, school size seems to affect teachers even more than students. A major shift seems to occur when a staff gets too large to sit down and plan together, to assume its rightful share of responsibility in setting a direction for the school. When this shift occurs, the best of our teachers, those who wish to take responsibility for professional decisions, find themselves in an intolerable situation. They have become nothing more than hired hands.

Teachers need to be convinced, of course, that any attempt to lead them into decision-making roles is not a subterfuge for manipulating

31

them. Unless they experience their power as genuine, they will resent the time wasted making pseudo-decisions. At the time of our visit, Gulliver's teachers had begun to resist the attempts of the principal to draw them into governance activities because they believed, rightly or wrongly, that he was engaged in a "con game." Little in our experience with the principal would lead us to a similar conclusion; rather, we found him generally open and forthright. It was the governance structure at Gulliver that contributed to such negative perceptions.

At Lilliput teachers talk little about governance activities, but they participate in them with willingness and energy. Besides all-school meetings, formal time is set aside at regular intervals for faculty meetings. All faculties have meetings, but few can experience the sort of power sharing we witnessed in a meeting of this small group of teachers. They feel involved in the day-to-day decisions required to run a school and, as a result, appear to have much greater commitment to its success.

Curricula and Programs

These two schools differ markedly in the curricula and programs they offer students. First, there are obvious differences in the size and diversity of the offerings. In one sense, Gulliver has broader and more diversified offerings in the staples of the American high school curriculum: English, mathematics, social studies, science, and foreign languages. There are also the usual courses in music, art, and physical education. Vocational education courses are available at a nearby school but require special scheduling for those who take them.

Gulliver is justifiably proud of its extracurricular offerings. Its students have won many awards for performances in music, fine arts, dramatics, and especially sports. Perhaps more than any other factor, these activities give the school its spirit and character.

Lilliput offers a much narrower curriculum in all the traditional high school subjects. Noticeably absent are large music performance groups and organized sports. However, Lilliput's students supplement its offerings by taking some courses at Gulliver or at the university. The existence of a major university a few blocks away and the availability of thousands of talented people in the community give Lilliput many opportunities to diversify and individualize its program. To its credit, it exploits these resources as well as any school we have seen.

Gulliver, only a few blocks farther from the university, views academic entanglements with the university as an administrative inconvenience and tends to limit them. Such entanglements would add yet one more level of complexity to an already complex structure. Although some students can and do take university courses as early as the summer after their sophomore year, this privilege is confined primarily to seniors. Apparently, university enrollment is limited to the number of people one counselor can supervise, even if demand is greater. For example, we talked to a junior who was in the advanced placement class for seniors, but he already had read all the material for even that level of work. When he asked permission to take a course at the university, he was told that this opportunity was open only to seniors, unless the class was at a time outside the school day. The student transferred to Lilliput and enrolled in the university class.

What we came to view as a paradox was how the two schools differed in the scope of their curricula. Our past experience with small high schools had led us to assume that the price one paid for a small-scale, informal atmosphere was a reduction in program. A handful of teachers could not be expected to offer the breadth of curriculum that a large, comprehensive high school with a staff of 100 teachers could offer. Lilliput contradicted that assumption. Lilliput's science teacher made reference to her advanced chemistry class. Since we knew she taught only part time at Lilliput, we assumed she was describing a class at Gulliver; she was not. By scavenging discarded equipment from Gulliver and the university, she had amassed enough resources to teach advanced chemistry at Lilliput. She told us that the poor quality of the equipment caused high errors of measurement in experiments, but she did not see that as a particular problem. Indeed, she believed the lab encouraged a good deal of ingenuity as students learned to construct various experiments with the limited equipment.

A key difference between these two faculties seems to be their definition of a minimal unit of instruction. At Gulliver, students told us that a class could not be offered unless there were 12 students interested in taking it. At Lilliput the minimal unit of instruction is the individual. A part-time Lilliput teacher told us that teachers find ways to meet students' needs. A student related this incident to us:

> A girl came to [the principal] and said, "I don't want to go to school. I hate school; I want to be a model." And he said, "Alright, let's see what we can do to help you do that as quickly as possible."

The girl had a program designed specifically for her, and she stayed in school. Several students at both schools related incidents of acquaintances who had transferred to Lilliput to pursue a program of study that was unavailable to them at Gulliver. These students no doubt were prompted to transfer not because the curriculum was irrelevant but because it was so inflexible.

Ironically, Lilliput, with its limited resources, is more able than Gulliver to foster scholarly experiences for a larger proportion of its students, despite the apparent advantage of Gulliver's large, well-trained, and specialized faculty. Gulliver's culture, with its emphasis on control and order, handicaps its curricular potential. While both schools encourage students' independent experiences, their difference in size influences the risks each school is ready to take with marginal scholars. Lilliput's small size allows it to manage problems with student progress in independent study, while Gulliver's large size poses problems of "things getting out of hand." Gulliver's staff may be justifiably wary of opening independent study to all takers.

Lilliput's scores on a battery of state evaluation instruments are very high. While these evaluations do not provide achievement data for individual students, they do provide composite data that form a profile of an entire school. The norm group for the percentile ranks used to report the results is comprised of essentially every high school in the state.

Lilliput's assessment scores, summarized in Table 1, were not only superior to Gulliver's scores but to those of virtually every other high school in the state. Lilliput does have smaller classes than Gulliver. It also has what many view as a more difficult group of students with which to work, a point acknowledged by one of Gulliver's assistant principals. Yet, when we discussed Lilliput's results with an evaluator in the state department of education, he discounted them as unrepresentative results because of the school's "specially selected, unusually talented student body." Can these two diametrically opposing views of this student body be correct, or are we confronted with a school culture so different that it renders even well-established norms invalid?

Tracking and Social Cliques

The reform reports suggest there is little value in the heavily tracked curricula found in most American high schools. We concur. Gulliver's multi-tracking does much to perpetuate many of the class distinctions found within the community and reinforces the cliques that exist among the students. A detailed description of Gulliver's cliques exposes the importance of these issues.

There are four major cliques and several minor ones that create a highly stratified society at Gulliver. The major cliques are the Brains,

Table 1. State Evaluation Scores for Gulliver and Lilliput.

| | Percentile Ranks | | | |
| | Gulliver | | Lilliput | |
Learning Goal	1981	1982	1981	1982
1. Self-Esteem	45	50	99	99
2. Understanding Others	55	80	99	99
3. Reading	75	99	99	99
4. Writing	80	95	99	99
5. Mathematics	95	99	99	99
6. Interest in School	65	80	99	99
7. Societal Responsibility	50	80	99	99
8. Knowledge of Law and Government	90	95	99	99
9. Health and Safety Practices	10	50	90	30
10. Creative Activities	85	90	99	95
11. Career Awareness	90	95	99	99
12. Appreciation of Human Accomplishments	65	75	99	99
13. Knowledge of Human Accomplishments	90	95	99	99
14. Information Usage	75	99	99	99
Mean Scores	69	84	98	94

the Jocks, the Hicks, and the Heads. Students, teachers, and administrators all seem to know them, usually by the same names. The cliques are a well-established way of life — more accurately, four different ways of life — within the school.

The Brains are the academically able students who are engaged in earnest preparations for college. They are serious students who are intellectually curious and work hard for high grades. According to one student's stereotype, they are the ones who wear "wire-rimmed glasses." Another student described a Brain as "someone who studies on the bus going on a field trip." Students seem not to make a conscious choice to be in this group, a factor less true of the other groups; they are simply acknowledged to be Brains because of the program in which they are enrolled and the unusual levels of conscientiousness they display. They often are ostracized because of their achievement orientation. We were unable to talk to many Brains (they had few study halls, which was our primary source for obtaining student interviews), and students we suspected to be Brains were usually unwilling to sacrifice study time to talk to us. Therefore we have little sense of their perceptions of the other groups.

The Jocks include many athletes, as their name implies, but this clique is not limited to them. It also includes cheerleaders and others deeply involved in the extracurricular life of the school. Another, and perhaps more descriptive term for this group would be the Socialites. The students in this group are active socially and, as one student put it, "They have higher, upper-class standards." Most have college aspirations. They try to do reasonably well academically, but that is not the main purpose for their being in this group. This distinction became clearer when we learned that the Preppies are a subgroup of the Jocks. The Preppies' primary interest, again according to stereotypes related to us, is in being seen in the "right" clothes and with the "beautiful" people.

Another major group, the Hicks, is comprised mostly of rural farm youths, though one teacher who works with them insisted that many live in town. For the most part, they are enrolled in vocational agriculture or vocational technical programs. Because many of them spend a half day at the high school and another half day at an area vocational high school, they are scheduled into the same set of classes at Gulliver; thus the school reinforces their group identity. The Hicks claim, for example, that they do not know about some of the activities of the school because announcements are usually made when they are not there. One teacher claimed that the vocational tech students (the Vo-Techers are a subset of the Hicks) are stigmatized as low-achieving kids. In her judgment, the portrayal is inaccurate.

The Heads are an invisible group of students who allegedly are the pushers and users of drugs. One teacher told us that a new student confided to her that drugs were more readily accessible than friends in the school. Apparently, the structure of cliques makes it difficult for a new student to break into these rigidly established groups. We learned less about the Heads than any of the other groups, perhaps because it is in their interest to remain invisible; but our hunch is that many nonconforming students are included in this classification, whether they use drugs or not.

Each clique distinguishes itself from the others by its manner of dress, the territory it occupies within the school, and by its lifestyle and habits. Apparently, in order to be identified with a clique, students have to wear the "uniform" for that group. For example, the Hicks are distinguished by their heavy boots, Levi jackets, and visored caps emblazoned with a farm-equipment logo.

In part, the cliques may be a product of the social class stratifications of the neighborhood elementary school, which in turn may reflect the stratification in the larger community. Our study was not designed to document this. Students reported to us that students from the same elementary school naturally banded together in junior high school.

The curriculum begins to evolve into separate tracks in junior high, the age when preadolescents begin to have concerns about identity. Social interests also emerge at this age, with sports becoming a more significant activity. All of these forces are amplified as students enter Gulliver. The cliques, which are mostly dormant in junior high, thrive on the incoming student's need to belong.

There is remarkably little interaction among the cliques, with each making conscious efforts to ignore the others. One student described the relationship as "tolerance" with an underlying current of "dislike." Others described the "tension" that exists between the groups. The interaction that does take place was invariably described in negative terms. Students from different cliques exchange "dirty looks," "verbal threats," and engage in name-calling. Fighting, once a more serious problem, has apparently decreased, perhaps as a consequence of the elimination of earlier overcrowded conditions. One student told us that her boyfriend had gotten into a fight with one of the Hicks the year before and "the entire Hick population got down on him. . . . They would walk down the halls and hit him." The situation became so bad that her friend finally transferred to Lilliput.

When students from one clique speak of the others, they use terms like "druggies," "dummies," "stuck ups," and "snobs." Resentment of the Jocks runs especially high among the Hicks. One Hick described them in this way:

> They live right in this general area [a "nice" section of town], and they just run around with each other all the time. Their fathers are big businessmen; they belong to the racquetball club, and stuff like that. They don't get to experience anything like we do. We go out in the fields and plow the fields and do a lot of activities in the country.

Another student said the Jocks were allowed to go into the courtyard during study halls because "they're goody-goodies" who "brown-nose the principal." A third said,

> They won't be so big and high and mighty when they try to get a job off one of us — when we own our own business. Then they'll have to be nice to us, and we won't have to be nice to them anymore.

A significant number of students do not identify with any of Gulliver's cliques. These students see themselves more as an aggregate of individuals than as another group. They interact with acquaintances in various cliques, but many of them speak of being isolated and lonely. When asked what it is like not being in a clique, a student responded, "It means you eat lunch alone, you walk to classes alone; you go outside alone, and say 'Hi' to a couple of people, and that's it." Another student added, "And sometimes at lunch you stand with them and talk with them, and at other times they just ignore you."

Students who do not ally themselves with a clique may be especially vulnerable to being ostracized. We talked to several students at Lilliput who left Gulliver largely because of student harassment. One slight young man related being forced into several fights because of his long hair. The final blow occurred when he emerged from a shower to find his clothes submerged in a basin of water. He was floundering at Lilliput because his learning style was really better served by the more structured classroom setting at Gulliver. Lilliput's principal estimated that there were about 20 students who had sought asylum in the program despite academic needs that likely would have been served better by Gulliver's more structured academic climate.

Students and teachers at Lilliput did not mention cliques very often; and when they did or when we asked about them, students described them as small friendship groups that did not exclude anyone. As one student stated, "We have cliques but they're not closed to other people or they don't cut down anybody or anything." Another student added, "It's more like a group of friends that decide that they like each other." A third student said,

> It doesn't mean that I can't come over and hang out with someone and talk to them. If I happen to wear designer jeans and they happen to be wearing cotton skirts, that's okay, you know. It's not closed; it's not even a clique; it's just like we're friends who hang out together.

A teacher confirmed,

> We don't have the strong cliques that [Gulliver] has. We do have cliques; but there's a lot more interaction [between them], and there's not the antagonism between certain cliques here [at Lilliput].

The distinction between tightly bound and loosely bound cliques is an important one, for the highly tolerant atmosphere of Lilliput encourages comparatively free and open communication between individuals and groups.

We offer three possible explanations for the extreme differences we saw in boundary setting in these two schools. One explanation is that the size of a school influences adolescents' concerns about personal identity. In a small school, one's identity can emerge out of the many interactions with others. The numerous opportunities for one-to-one interactions with adults who see this as an important facet of their job is probably significant to their development. Lilliput's environment is a very friendly and supportive one, an environment conducive to exploring and constructing a unique identity.

A second possibility is that the larger, more impersonal environment of the typical American high school is not so much harsh or hostile as it is uncertain. In such an environment, adolescents have difficulty constructing a comfortable identity. Perhaps at Gulliver the cliques give students a relatively safe and easy way to acquire an instant identity that, if not acceptable to everyone, is acknowledged as legitimate by sufficiently large numbers of peers to establish one's selfhood.

Yet a third explanation is that Lilliput has no tightly bound cliques because it has a more homogeneous group of students. Tolerance is a much easier virtue to attain when the range of values to be tolerated is narrow. At Gulliver the Jocks and Hicks are the two most antagonistic factions. Indeed, besides establishing the rules of membership in their own groups, they seem to be the prime definers of the other groups in the school, perhaps because of their sheer size. We sensed that some of their members take comfort in being able to summarize this intricate social fabric in such simple terms; it seems to make their world manageable. This mechanism clearly is not a healthy way to develop toward adulthood; because cliques do more to retard personal growth than they do to foster it, they work against Gulliver's efforts in this area.

According to Goodlad (1984), several of the goals of schooling are to develop social, civic, and cultural competence. Gulliver's hidden curriculum, especially the message conveyed by its system of tracking, teaches values (for example, intolerance for others) that are inimical to those in the formal curriculum. We do not believe that simply eliminating tracking would dissolve these cliques; they are a product of the scale of the school and the stratification of the community that is only reinforced by Gulliver's curriculum.

Personal Meaning

These two schools also differ in the extent to which they attempt to help students make sense of their world. "Relevance" has become a cliche, but the pedagogical importance of the concept has not diminished. Even the reformers, particularly Goodlad and Sizer, stress it.

The informal environmnent that is possible in a small school fosters the development of personal meaning. Values can be clarified through discussion and personal contacts. The content-oriented, formal curriculum of a large school is not well suited to this goal. To construct personal meanings through the curriculum, students must be actively involved in probing and reflecting on the issues under discussion. While Gulliver's teachers undoubtedly lead some excellent discussions, the informal opportunities to pursue a point or extend thinking are limited for most students. The general climate of the school, with its tight schedules and lack of time for individual contact between students and teachers, robs both groups of such rich opportunities.

Character Education

That Lilliput's teachers are concerned with character education is clear, though they do not call it that. It was evident in at least two ways in the formal curriculum and supported by the educational philosophy of the school.

In the formal curriculum of the school, there is a period devoted to a wide variety of activities that occur in small, established groups called "Clumps." Similar to the old homeroom concept in some respects, Clumps provide a formally scheduled opportunity about once each month for students and teachers to interact at length free of the burden of covering subject matter. During Clump days, these small groups meet to see a film, debate an issue, discuss some aspect of school life, or offer assistance to one of their members. Sometimes they simply go on a picnic together. When the school considered adding seventh- and eighth-grade students to its student body, the Clumps provided one forum for students to air their concerns about the change.

Clumps are not therapy groups led by untrained leaders, as critics of such programs have charged. They engage in a wide variety of activities and deal with a variety of issues and concerns: the environment, nuclear energy, women's rights, humane treatment of domestic animals, the killing of whales, and so on. They function more as a diversified assembly program carried out in discussion-size groups.

The Clumps are supplemented by teachers being available to students throughout the day. The college-type schedule of this open-campus school permits teachers to respond to individual students on a regular basis. Much of the activity during these times is based on classroom or subject matter issues, but a good portion is given to the personal issues raised by students or to just talking about world events. The informality of these contacts erodes the usual barriers between students and teachers.

These two vehicles, Clumps and open scheduling, sustain an educational philosophy that values increased and more informal contact between teachers and students. Besides giving teachers another avenue for discovering student interests and needs, informal contact is educative in other ways. For example, a point that is made as a follow-up to a classroom discussion may sink in more readily when it is offered in this informal way.

But how do these vehicles for informal, affective education build character? First, they permit teachers to serve as role models to students as they work through the problems of growing up. They also give teachers numerous opportunities to address without preaching such issues as responsible behavior, tolerance for others, honesty, and hard work, and, more importantly, without embarrassing a student in front of peers. These matters can be addressed naturally in the circumstances in which they arise.

The point is that when schools are able to make a serious effort to build a sense of community among all of their participants and to incorporate a commitment to individuals in both the curriculum and other aspects of school life, the entire environment encourages the achievement of character goals. A sense of community can be far more than the rah-rah spirit of a football rally. It is caring about the needs and interests of the other members of the community, whether they are students or teachers. This becomes possible within a structure that makes acting on these needs and interests a natural process.

Control

One of the major differences between these two schools is the levels of control they exercise. Gulliver is in no way an oppressive environment. Were we not sensitized to control issues by the testimony of its students and by the contrasting experience at Lilliput, we might have overlooked the issues. But because of the contrast, we came to see the degree to which control issues affected every aspect of the school.

Most Gulliver teachers viewed control in terms of accountability and responsibility. As one teacher put it:

> I may be old-fashioned, but I think kids need direction. They need
> to be somewhere, accountable for some reason. They need some-
> one to tell them.

This view of students as needing external direction in order to function effectively as learners was a common theme. Many Gulliver
teachers appeared sincere in their belief that Gulliver students were
not mature enough to handle much freedom and responsibility. Gulliver's teachers did not mention self-discipline as a goal. If asked, they
would surely have been in favor of it. (Who can be against self-
discipline?) Our sense of the situation is that they generally believe
that most teenagers are incapable of it. In the context of a large high
school, they are probably right. A large high school probably is incapable of fostering self-discipline, and Gulliver would be wasting its time
in trying to foster it. A faculty, quite reasonably, may assume that self-
discipline is something that develops naturally with maturity; it is
"caught" rather than "taught."

At Lilliput control tends to be viewed as a developmental issue rather than as a security problem. Teachers are concerned about providing a supportive environment in which students can acquire the skills
and attitudes of self-control. In this sense, control is more of a pedagogical issue at Lilliput than it is at Gulliver. As one teacher told us:

> I see us intentionally set up to insure that just about every kid
> has access to an adult who, for the most part, has good judgment. . . .
> We do a lot to support kids because we're smaller and almost ev-
> ery staff member has a chance to meet every kid. . . . We get to
> see the little changes, the little developmental things.

Most Lilliput students held a similar view, as shown by the following
exchange:

> Interviewer: Do you find that it's easy to goof off because you are
> on your own?
>
> Mary: Yeah, it is. It's very hard when you're downtown or some-
> thing and you have a class and people are saying, "Come on,
> let's do whatever," and you know you have a class and you're
> not sure you should go back. . . . You know you should, but you
> don't know if you want to.
>
> Jim: It just takes discipline, self-discipline.
>
> Mary: Yeah, definitely. You have to have a lot of self-discipline,
> but if you can do it, it's great.
>
> Jim: And the school helps administer a little self-discipline if you
> get behind. Like I started skipping classes a lot, and the teacher

and my parents and me had an emergency counseling session
where we talked about it, and then I stopped skipping.

Gulliver's students see control and order almost exclusively in terms
of restrictions (something being imposed on them), deprivation (the
removal of privileges and the loss of freedom), or punishment.

> Jill: I think they're a little too rough. Like they won't let you go
> out to lunch. School lunches are okay, but they're not great;
> and sometimes I like to go out to lunch.
>
> Interviewer: That's a recent change, isn't it? Why was that change
> made — from an open to a closed campus?
>
> Bob: People were abusing their rights. It was kind of hard, when
> people were leaving school and stuff, to keep track of them;
> and a lot of kids just wouldn't come back for their classes.
>
> Interviewer: Going out and just not coming back?
>
> Bob: Skipping class and stuff. And they figured it made it a lot
> easier keeping everyone in the building so they could keep track
> of them.

The closing of the campus two years prior to our study presented
an interesting situation for the analysis of control. The change was
forced, in part, because of parental pressure. Since all of the reference
groups (students, teachers, and administrators) compared control issues across the two eras, we had an excellent basis for understanding
their attitudes toward control. Moreover, because Lilliput still had an
open campus, we could compare and contrast the attitudes of teachers,
administrators, and students in each school.

During the open-campus period, Gulliver's students were permitted
to leave the school grounds for lunch and at other times when they
did not have class. Moreover, they were not required to attend study
halls. Gulliver now requires students to remain on the school grounds
during the school day unless they have written permission to leave.
A written request by parents is required unless the student is 18, in
which case the student can make the request directly. Students also
are required to be in assigned study halls.

Gulliver's teachers agree with the return to the closed campus. One
teacher put it this way:

> I don't know whether they [the students] changed in their attitudes
> — the way they look at the school — but I do see a change. Things
> are quieter around here since they initiated the closed study hall.

Another teacher described the lack of responsibility when Gulliver had an open campus.

> During the open-campus period, students were permitted to congregate in the lobby if they had a study hall. They could go to the cafeteria; they could go to the library; they could move around; they were not responsible for their actions — really — I mean as far as having to be somewhere.

One teacher thought that the shift to a closed campus came none too soon.

> I felt, at one time, that the school was going to blow up. They [the students] had set fire to a bulletin board and one girl had her hair set on fire. . . . I had a great fear that something really drastic was going to happen.

Except for one or two other references to vandalism, this was the only teacher with whom we talked who viewed the lack of control as a safety threat to persons in the school.

Most of Gulliver's students whom we interviewed resented being punished for someone else's mistakes; they believed (teachers and administrators agreed) that it was a small minority of students who were unable to handle the increased freedom and responsibility that the open campus required. The students disliked the return to the closed campus with its mandatory study halls, its restrictions on leaving the building, and the security guards who patrolled the school's grounds; they likened it to "being in prison." The guards were a visible symbol of the restrictions now imposed on their lives.

Students, teachers, and the principal at Lilliput take a different view of their open campus, illustrated by the following dialogue with students:

> Interviewer: You mentioned that the community views this school as a weird place. I've been in a lot of alternative schools around the country and a lot of times the community is concerned with something it calls "control", and they see alternatives as out-of-control places. Would you comment on whether you feel there is control in your school and, if so, what it is.
>
> Mary: I think a lot of people consider they have control over kids when they lock them in a building for seven hours, and I just think that's crazy. You don't give them responsibility; you keep them in a building and make them go to study halls when they could have free time.
>
> George: Control is directly related to honesty in student-teacher relationships, and the amount of control a student senses is

44

trying to be inflicted on him relates to how honest he's going to be about what he's actually doing. At [Lilliput], there is less control; and you can say to your teacher, "I've got a problem. I went out and did this and this," and most likely the teacher will say, "Well, that's a problem. Why did you do it?". . . They're looking for the problem, not just treating symptoms.

Ann: People say there's bad control at [Lilliput], but I think it's just not as apparent as it is at [Gulliver]. At [Gulliver] people are either in classes or in study hall, and there's nobody in the hallways at any time during the day. At [Lilliput] you can go wherever you want as long as you don't have a class. But if you start screwing up, then you hear about it. If I started skipping my classes and stuff like that, then a meeting would be called with my parents and teachers to decide what the problem is and not just give detention. . . . It's like you have as much responsibility as you can handle; and if you can't handle it, it's taken away from you for a while. But you start out having it.

One Lilliput teacher addressed the issue of control this way:

I think we have some new students coming to us that are not really sure quite how to act. I think they have to be educated towards that cooperative attitude rather than that control attitude.

Both schools report few instances of such serious problems as fighting, vandalism, stealing, and drug abuse. Apparently, about two years before our study, fighting was a problem at Gulliver. One administrator attributed the reduction in the number of fights to "taking a pretty tough stance on kids fighting." The school's expulsion proceedings against seven students who eventually withdrew is one example of that stance.

The incidence of fighting was also quite low at Lilliput. As one student said,

One strange thing about the school is we've never had a fight. In the existence of the school, there's never been a real fight here.

While the statement has the ring of exaggeration, fighting clearly was not an issue in the school.

Knowing where kids are, a problem identified by Gulliver's staff, was not mentioned at Lilliput. This does not mean that Lilliput's teachers are not interested in the whereabouts of their students, but suggests a willingness to trust that students are not up to mischief wherever they are. When inappropriate behavior occurs, the Lilliput staff does deal with it; but it does not try to prevent it through tight surveillance. Gulliver is much more likely to want to know where students are in

45

order to prevent misbehavior from occurring and, perhaps additionally, in response to its sense of accountability to the community. This community, like many, probably views control as a fundamental task of Gulliver and views low levels of control as mismanagement.

Two Cultures

That two such very different schools can operate in the sociopolitical framework that is American public education is heartening. New forms of the high school *can* be implemented, given a modicum of courage and insight on the part of a community's policy makers. We trust that point is clear from the foregoing discussion. What is less easy to convey are the differences in the sense of personal involvement and commitment we felt repeatedly in conversations with students and teachers in the two schools. Lilliput is not Utopia, but its problems tend to be "owned" by its entire school community rather than attributed to some segment of it.

The next two chapters consider why personal involvement and commitment occur with such apparent ease in a small school and why it seems so remote a possibility in even a modest-sized high school staffed by talented, well-meaning people such as is the case at Gulliver. Chapter 3 considers theories and research on culture, particularly as they apply to the sense of community in school settings. Chapter 4 reiterates many of the themes introduced in Chapters 1 and 2, describing how they manifest themselves in numerous small high schools across the country.

Chapter 3
Community and Culture

The school community develops distinctive normative pat-
terns that draw students toward or away from particular ac-
tivities and domains of development (social, academic, and
physical). These normative patterns will have a profound long-
term effect on the self-concepts, values, and skills that will be
developed. Personalities will interact with the social system
productively or unproductively with long-term effects on moti-
vation and learning styles. The modulating capability of the
school environment will have much to do with whether or not
that interaction will be productive. Finally, homes and neigh-
borhoods impart their distinctive patterns and these, too, will
interact productively or unproductively with the environment
of the school. The school's ability to capitalize and compensate
will, again, be responsible for whether the interaction is
productive.

—Bruce Joyce, Richard Hersh, and
Michael McKibbin (1983, p. 114)

There is no such thing as a high school without a culture, just as there
are no individuals without personalities. But the cultures of two high
schools can be as different as the personalities of two individuals. It
is difficult to grasp in concrete terms the meaning of such a phrase
as "the culture of a high school." Yet we talk about "the American people" or "young girls" or "retirees" as groups that share some general
traits. Similarly, we can talk about high school cultures.

47

An institution's culture and subcultures may be defined by its symbols, norms or patterns of behavior, and basic beliefs and values. The culture of schools includes lesson plans, units of instruction, tests, grading, remediation, evaluation, and other facets of schooling. It also includes such elements as control, discipline, reward and punishment, movement, time, and individual responsibility.

The norms or patterns of behavior in high schools have been described in rich detail. For example, Lortie (1975) provides much empirical data on the patterns of teacher behavior. Teachers talk much more than do their students; they are in front of the room a great deal; they speak to individuals and to the group as a whole, providing direction for the activities of the classroom. Their role is both proscriptive and prescriptive, setting expectations and guiding behavior. Student behavior has its patterns as well. Moving from class to class, getting seated before the bell rings, responding to the teacher's questions, and doing various kinds of seatwork are a few of these patterns.

Barker and Gump (1964) describe the behavior of teachers and students in terms of the physical setting and materials of the room. The students' desks face forward toward the teacher and the chalkboard. The desks have tablet arms permitting students to take notes from the chalkboard or the teacher's oral presentation. Sometimes the desks are pushed into circles to discuss some topic or issue. The unscrewing of the desks from the floor symbolically reflects a shifting philosophy of education from one with communication only between teacher and student to one with more extensive interaction.

Most large high schools are heavily oriented toward control. Students are watched carefully. They are not allowed to wander alone or in small groups. Their behavior is corrected when it gets out of hand. Discipline is viewed less as a goal to be attained, in the sense of self-discipline, than as something to be meted out when a student has violated behavior norms.

A school's culture includes a system of beliefs and values providing an invisible framework for the behavior of both students and teachers. What schooling is believed to be has a great deal to do with how it is carried out, and how it is carried out reinforces this system of beliefs and values. According to Dreeben (1968), schooling is not only internally consistent (beliefs are congruent with behavior), but it also is consistent with the broader values of the larger society. The culture of the school is a mirror image, though sometimes a distorted one, of the culture within which it functions. Dreeben suggests, for example, that schools help children make the transition from the more intimate values of the family to the more impersonal values of the larger society. They do this by teaching norms of independence (doing your own work), achievement (getting the job done), universalism (treating everyone alike), and specificity (emphasizing detail). Beliefs and values such as these are conveyed as much through the attitudes and actions of the hidden curriculum of schooling as through the formal curriculum.

An illustration provides a more concrete meaning for how values influence behavior. One concept of professionalism is that professionals must maintain a certain social distance between themselves and their clients (students). According to this view, social distance permits the professional to be objective in evaluating needs and delivering services. Accordingly, those who hold this view "distance" themselves by using titles (Dr., Mr., Ms., etc.), by wearing clothing that is different from the client (we even speak of dressing professionally), by reserving certain equipment and facilities for their exclusive use (no students allowed), and by restricting informal contact between themselves and their clients. This view of a professional is embedded in our culture and specifically in the subculture of schooling.

During the 1960s a different view of professional behavior emerged, not only within education but in other fields as well. According to this view, a professional must know the client as intimately as feasible within the time constraints available. According to this view, a teacher can not really teach a student effectively without knowing the student's needs, interests, and talents in detail; and such knowledge can only be obtained through close personal contact. Using first names, wearing similar clothes, and providing equal access to facilities were some of the ways used to break down the barriers of social convention. Public alternative schools, which generally attract younger teachers who dress like their students and are more egalitarian in their values and behavior, embody this newer definition of professionalism. The curriculum, governance, and social climate complement this definition of a professional. This whole panoply of differences constitutes a culture of schooling very different from that normally associated with the high school. Similar trends have taken place in nursing, medicine, law, and other fields.

There is evidence to suggest that such developments represent an attempt by a major segment of our society to resist the trend toward a more impersonal world. Naisbitt (1984) has observed that every recent technological breakthrough has been accompanied by a corresponding emphasis on human intimacy, what he calls the high-tech, high-touch phenomenon. Small scale, informal organizations have flourished in this new context.

A Sense of Community

A very important — probably the most important — segment of a school's culture is the degree to which all its inhabitants see themselves as one group that collaborates to make the school work, that is, the extent to which they experience a sense of community.

In Chapter 2, we discussed how American education tries to respond to two basic but, in some ways, conflicting values: individuality, by which a school strives to enhance the unique talents, interests, and skills of each individual; and community, by which a school strives to develop a sense of belonging to a group and of feeling some commitment to it. Stone and Wehlage (1982), building on the work of Berlak and Berlak (1980), have examined such value conflicts.

Conflict exists because two values that are, in important respects, inherently opposing are nevertheless both prized. The decisions, conscious or unconscious, personal or professional, that an individual or a group makes in an attempt to strike a balance between these opposing values have a profound influence on the social climate of a school. Typically, such decisions are culturally determined; and they define, among other characteristics, the sense of community a school develops.

If culture is the complex web of elements that constitute a way of life, then community is the essence of that way of life. Culture is analogous to an atom with community as its nucleus. Community is the binding force that draws the people of a culture into a more or less harmonious interactive network.

All high schools have some degree of community. Teachers and students sense that they are engaged in a common enterprise. They rally around some common symbols (the band or the football team), and they assist one another in reaching some common goals. But in most high schools, as we saw in Gulliver High, the emphasis on community is not particularly strong, as reflected by the presence of student cliques, alienation, and a lack of tolerance for different values. The typical high school is better understood as an aggregate — a loosely knit collection of individuals — than as a community. In organizational terms, the people and units are loosely coupled, each interacting just enough with the others to achieve his or her own isolated purposes. The organizational purposes also get met, but not as neatly or as fully as most of us would like.

The teachers and students in most high schools do not deliberately resist becoming communities, but neither do they make much of an effort to develop a strong community. Sporadic, brief contacts that lack intensity inhibit the development of a sense of community. Contacts between the key subgroups (students and teachers) are limited by the physical surroundings of the school, the tightly scheduled and task-oriented day, and the curricular constraints of the program. Interactions between students and teachers lack much personal meaning or significance. In the name of a common purpose — progressing through what has come to be defined as a high school education — routines take over, preventing adults and the young from establishing much in common. No one actively seeks the result, but almost all passively accept it.

We tend to recognize communities by how *distinctive* they are from the rest of society. The Amish community brings to mind visions of people dressed in dark clothing, riding in horse-drawn carriages, who speak in their own language and set themselves apart from other people. Among other factors, then, a community has its separateness, the ways in which it defines itself as different from other people who may interact with it. These differences are important elements of its identity.

Communities may differ in the dress of their people, the language their people use, the intensity of their interactions, and the nature of their interactions with outsiders. Habits and lifestyles help the people in a community to feel that they are distinctive.

Also imbedded in the concept of community is the idea of a *sense of purpose*. People in a community may live their lives in a unique way because they feel some special purpose will be served by doing so. Monks believe they are devoting their lives to God; the Amish believe they are carrying on the traditions of their forefathers. Communities do not have to be religious to have a sense of purpose. Many communes were established in the Sixties in which people set themselves apart from the modern world and its hectic pace. Their inhabitants wanted to return to a simpler, self-sufficient lifestyle, tied to the land. Whether religious or not, a group of people has to have a sense of purpose if it is to think of itself as a community.

A third characteristic of communities is *commitment*. People in special communities either develop a sense of commitment or eventually leave. Commitment implies a belief in the values and traditions of the community. Usually, there are a small number of core values that form the belief structure of each community. These values cannot be

51

breached if people wish to be treated as continuing members of the community. In the event that the values are breached, the transgressor may be ostracized or treated as a marginal member of the community. Eventually, if the treatment continues, he or she is likely to leave. Some high school dropouts follow this pattern. Perhaps the values espoused by the school are generally in conflict with those of the student, and eventually the student learns this and refuses to give up his or her own values. The only recourse left to the student is to leave school.

Individuals join groups and continue to participate in them because these groups meet their basic needs for dependence, affiliation, power, achievement, and so on. Individuals are likely to have their needs met when the culture of the group more nearly matches their own beliefs and values, and this is more likely to be true when they have had an opportunity to participate in the development and articulation of those values. When the match between the individual's values and the community's values is close, a strong link is forged between the two. The community contributes to the shaping of the individual, who, in turn, participates in the molding of the community.

Healthy and Unhealthy Communities

Not all communities are healthy for the individuals in them. A street gang, for example, may be a very strong community, but the values of the community are in serious conflict with those of society. At one level, the gang may improve a member's circumstances; he may be safer on the streets. At another level, the community he has chosen places him in great physical jeopardy. In sum, the gang can be judged an unhealthy community.

It may not be accurate to say that high schools are unhealthy places for students and teachers; but in many large high schools there is little sense of community. Many schools have the potential of becoming healthy communities, but that potential is largely unrealized, a point to which we will return.

The concept of wellness is useful in this context. We typically understand health as the absence of illness. When we are ill we know something is wrong. We take medication and rest to return to a normal state of health, but our normal state of health may be relatively unhealthy. We may smoke too much, drink too much, be overweight, and exercise too little. In other words, our normal state of health is considerably less healthy than it could be. Wellness requires us to go beyond not being ill. To achieve it, we must eat properly, exercise, and do the other things that we know will bring us to a higher state of health. The parallels with high schools are clear. The reform reports, whether one agrees with their specific recommendations or not, are trying to return schools to their "normal" state of health. Our argument is that such an action is not good enough. We must not aim for an institution that is not sick but for one that is well. If high schools can develop a sense of community — a bond of commitment between students and teachers — they will be taking a significant step toward a state of wellness.

We can sense differences when we visit a variety of high schools. We know when teachers and students are smiling and friendly and try to be helpful, we have a positive feeling about the school. While these first impressions may or may not be accurate, they do suggest that a concept like institutional wellness is part of our everyday understanding.

The characteristics that define communities as having a strong sense of wellness are caring, commitment, and trust, which build strong bonds between individuals in the community; and physical, mental, and emotional support, which enable individuals to risk, succeed, and grow.

Community and the Goals of Schooling

A sense of community functions independently of other school outcomes, such as academic achievement, although it may be related to one or more of them. Does a sense of community really contribute to student learning? While it could well make a difference as to whether students learn, that should not be the primary concern. Rather, a healthy sense of community should be an important goal in its own right. It should be pursued because a healthy environment that encourages healthy individuals is important in and of itself. By contrast, a poor sense of community can impair achievement if it is severe enough to cause students to not want to come to school or even to drop out.

An example may clarify the point. Lewin, Lippitt, and White (1939) studied the effects of different leadership styles on the behavior of 10-year-old boys. Each leadership style created very different social climates. They concluded that while authoritarian leaders (and climates) are more productive on some occasions than democratic ones, the negative side effects of the climates they create — aggression, hostility, and apathy — are also high. In one experiment, hostility directed

53

at objects or peers was 30 times more prevalent in the authoritarian groups than in the democratic ones. Thus productivity must be balanced against the personal and social consequences.

Risk, Support, and Growth

It is clear that our world is changing at a dramatic rate and that these changes challenge our existing beliefs and values. The family, an institution under great stress, offers few opportunities for the young to obtain emotional support in a warm and caring environment. Communes and cult groups provide this kind of support to thousands of young people starving for such attention. Women's support groups and suicide hot lines provide support to other portions of the population. Established communities used to serve these functions but no longer seem to do so.

Schools that have developed a strong sense of community are attractive to their students. Students want to attend them because they offer, through caring teachers and fellow students, the physical, mental, and emotional support that all of us need.

> *Item:* Students at one high school demonstrated their support for a student who had been irregular in his attendance by driving to his home to encourage him to attend.

It is out of visible acts of caring such as this that communities are created.

A supportive environment must not be "smothering" in its support; it must walk the fine line between providing support and encouraging independence. For students to risk, they must be independent enough to attempt a task and secure in knowing that failure is manageable, that is, sufficient support will be there if it is needed. An environment without risk is not conducive to growth, and growth is what high schools are supposed to be about. The high school must find ways to bring challenging experiences into its curriculum if it is to provide meaningful experiences to the young and those who teach them. Because schools with a strong sense of community are warm and supportive environments, students can be encouraged to take risks and accept failure. As they take each step toward independence and self-sufficiency, they know that support will be there for them should they need it.

Authority Structures in Communities

How does authority function in schools with a strong sense of community? First, authority is not imposed by the hierarchical structure of the school system. Top-down authority of this sort is at cross-purposes with the nature of a community. In communities the authority of the group replaces the authority of the hierarchy in controlling the beliefs and behavior of its individual members. Norms evolve out of the everday life of the group, representing what it values. If freedom of speech is valued in a group, its norms will express that value. If students are thought to be irresponsible, the norms will permit little movement without surveillance.

In a small high school with a strong sense of community, authority to control behavior emerges out of the interaction of individuals on a daily basis. Individuals in a community shape the values by which it functions. Egalitarian values often dominate this shaping process in small high schools. The process is an evolving one, which is simply to say that learning is going on. The adults (and some students) struggle to establish a firm understanding of what constitutes appropriate behavior with those still testing their newfound power. Negotiation and refinement are ongoing activities — between adult and young, one individual and another, and one individual and the group.

The authority of a community is strengthened by the shared values of its members. Internal cohesion is substituted for external authority as a device for controlling student and teacher behavior. The more cohesion, the greater the sense of unity and the firmer hold the group has on its members. Swidler (1979) reinforces the point:

> Certain organizations such as intentional communities and some social movements, reverse the usual relationship between peer ties and organizational control. These organizations manage to harness peer loyalties so that they contribute to organizational goals. (p. 97)

The ideal, of course, is to foster organizational goals and individual goals through the same activities. Under such circumstances, the needs of both the individual and the group are met.

Schools as Unrealized Communities

A sense of community is largely stillborn in many large high schools. No one may resist it, and many may be working toward it; but it remains largely unrealized. In such schools, there are usually a set of symptoms that signal the underlying problem.

Depersonalization and Alienation. Social commentators point to the terrible toll that alienation takes on our young. Many youngsters come to high school alienated and depersonalized and find little assistance there to help them cope with alienation. Indeed, high schools often reinforce isolation and loneliness in the structures they create.

Newmann (1981) points out the relationship between students' alienation and their lack of involvement in schools. He asserts that active participation by students in all aspects of school life can counteract the alienation that many feel. We posit a different explanation. We think the emotional isolation results from a failure of community, and that a lack of participation is a symptom of alienation. A greater sense of community stimulates increased participation. At that point, Newmann's thesis comes in to play: As a higher level of involvement in the life of the school (in its community) develops, alienation dissolves.

Repression. When judged by objective standards, most high schools are repressive places. But it is a soft form of repression and thus less likely to provoke significant resistance. Silberman documents this feeling in *Crisis in the Classroom* (1970), and the film *High School* (Weisman 1968) captures it starkly. Repressive institutions are control oriented. Without control, so the reasoning goes, there is imminent danger; control tames the wild beast in humans that is searching to get out. Not all control is repressive, but all control can lead to repression. Our own research (Smith and Gregory 1985) documents this factor of control in high schools (though not necessarily repression). We found that teachers and students in a large high school saw their school as placing heavy emphasis on security in order to "keep the lid on."

Repression feeds alienation and feelings of powerlessness; students feel they have little power to change things. Ironically, teachers also feel this sense of powerlessness. According to Nirenberg (1977), teachers in more bureaucratic schools have less power and autonomy; they, too, feel helpless to make a difference.

Apathy and Boredom. High schools often are boring places for students and for teachers as well. When young children start school, they usually love it and look forward to going. As they grow older, they become more and more dissatisfied with their school experience. What is the cause of this disaffection?

One factor is that the school's curriculum is perceived as less meaningful by many youngsters. The connections between what they do in school and what they do with their lives outside of school become increasingly obscure. Silberman (1970) and the annual Phi Delta Kappa/Gallup Polls of the Public's Attitudes Toward the Public Schools have documented boredom and apathy as problems for decades. The single most important problem that student leaders identify in their high schools is not drugs, not discipline, but apathy (McQuigg and Smith 1985). Apathy and boredom are the twin killers of an active mind. They are signs of a failure of community.

Structures as Obstacles. The structures of the high school are not functional. They promote neither learning nor community. They promote isolation, formalism, competition, and intolerance. As Husen (1985) points out, schools are suffering from "the combined affliction of meritocracy and bureaucracy" (p. 398). Meritocracy pits the gifted-and-talented against the mentally retarded; those in between are largely ignored. What becomes of an average, hard-working student in such a climate?

> *Item:* A large high school in Illinois, often cited for its unusually large annual crop of National Merit Scholarship finalists, also has an alarmingly high teenage suicide rate.

Schools have, in large measure, ignored the motivating power of a strong sense of community. Such schools have little hold on their students and teachers. Teachers head for the door at the end of their last class, and students drop out — in many ways. Community is not rejected; it is never tried. Thousands of such "normal" schools exist throughout the country.

That high schools are largely unrealized communities is not surprising. Many forces pull them toward impersonality: size, complexity, lack of commitment, weakened parental and public ties. That teachers, students, and administrators work together as well as they do is to their credit. The room for improvement, however, is vast. The key step to rectifying the situation is a reduction in the size of high schools. Size, more than any other factor, impedes the development of community.

But why community? It may help people feel good about themselves, but what does it do beyond that? For one thing, it provides a unifying force; it increases commitment among students and teachers; it lessens alienation and improves motivation; it gives teachers greater autonomy and harnesses the human potential that is in every social situation; and it gives students a greater stake in a school and increases their identification with it. Without community, school is just a place to get through as painlessly as possible; with community, it is *our* school, a place in which to live and find meaning.

One of the shortcomings of the reform reports is that they focus almost exclusively on curriculum content and pedagogy. These are worthwhile goals, but they cannot replace the need for a broader vision of education. The Latin root of education, *educere,* literally means to "lead out." One cannot lead anyone anywhere without their consent, without the leader developing a strong bond or relationship with the led. In a recent book, Bennis and Nanus (1985) make a distinction between managers and leaders: "Managers are people who do things right and leaders are people who do the right things" (p. 21). The reform reports focus on doing things right. In contrast, developing a strong sense of community is one of those right things to do.

Chapter 4

The Case for Small High Schools

Most education occurs in small, close communities, such as the family (both nuclear and extended), the neighborhood, and the small workplace with its apprentices. In urban, bureaucratized society, more attention is paid to superficial qualities of individuals than to deeper character traits, which can be discovered only through close and prolonged contact. This is also true of schooling, and any attempt to come to grips with today's troubled schools must consider how to establish more self-directed schools with closer ties to parents and to the surrounding community.

—Torsten Husen (1985, p. 402)

[T]he program [of a small high school] works to reveal rather than conceal all kinds of social and motivational problems of the students. It does more than that. Having exposed the difficulties, the school provides mechanisms for resolving them. Where the issue is strictly personal, individual advising and support groups are available. Where the issue is communal, the advising groups and Governance provide forums for resolution. The use of these mechanisms gives students a feeling that the school is a dynamic place, always changing to correct itself. And both teachers and students are convinced that they have a strong voice in the decisions that are made. Thus both groups express a strong sense of pride and ownership in the program.

—Bert Horwood (1983, p. 80)

The large high schools that have developed over the past few decades would not have evolved if they did not offer certain advantages and economies. We shall challenge these purported advantages as we build the case for small high schools. Some of our arguments are not new. Dewey's Utopian School (1933) would have had 200 students. Schumacher, in *Small Is Beautiful* (1975), stresses the importance of maintaining a balance in the scale of our institutions and processes. He argues for the need to adjust the serious imbalance in the size of our institutions:

> Today, we suffer from an almost universal idolatry of giantism. It is therefore necessary to insist on the virtues of smallness — where this applies. (If there were a prevailing idolatry of smallness, irrespective of subject or purpose, one would have to try and exercise influence in the opposite direction.)
>
> The question of scale might be put in another way: what is needed in all these matters is to discriminate, to get things sorted out. For every activity there is a certain appropriate scale, and the more active and intimate the activity, the smaller the number of people that can take part, the greater is the number of such relationship arrangements that need to be established. (p. 66)

Learning is an active process and, at its richest, an intimate one. It thrives in supportive settings with a sense of community.

Barker and Gump (1964) found levels of participation of students in small high schools (under 150 students) three to 20 times greater than in the largest high school (almost 2,300 students) they studied. Although they found a more limited curriculum in their small high schools, it should be noted that they were studying small high schools that were established as little comprehensive high schools. In other words, these small high schools generally functioned under what we will term the handicap of a large-school structure.

Our argument for small high schools makes no sense unless they can mount academic programs that are at least as effective, if very different, as those of large, comprehensive high schools. We started building that case in Chapter 2 and will continue it later, but in this chapter we will concentrate on high schools as places in which to build a sense of community.

Small high schools have some obvious advantages as communities; but these are potential, not inherent, advantages. Indeed, high schools are often of a size that we consider optimum and yet have communities as underdeveloped as large schools. These schools regularly share two characteristics of their larger brethren. They have adopted a large-school structure that tends to separate people rather than bring them together, and they lack a commonly shared idea of what the school is striving to become. Each of these concepts deserves some attention.

Status influences the course of education in many ways. Schools arrange themselves in a pecking order; small high schools have sought to emulate large high schools. In recent decades, a school was immediately on the defensive if it did not have all the facilities and specialized personnel that a large school had. James Conant's influential book, *The American High School Today* (1959), preyed on these insecurities. Small schools — those with graduating classes of less than 100 students — were considered inherently inferior because they could not offer as many foreign languages or advanced science courses. As long as the instructional model was one teacher working with 25 or 30 students, one needed lots of students to be able to hire lots of teachers with lots of different specialties. In addition, if one saw the primary, perhaps sole, purpose of school to be the transmission of content, the case became compelling. One did what one could to become a large school. Several small schools in a sparsely populated area would consolidate. To the costs of new bricks and mortar, one could add increased ennui and anonymity for students and a heightened isolation for teachers. One of the investments a child might make to get advanced chemistry was an additional 200 hours a year wasted riding a school bus to a larger but more distant school, more distant both geographically and personally.

If consolidation was not feasible, one did what one could to emulate a large school's organization and curriculum. Departmentalizing a faculty might occur even if the resulting "department" numbered three faculty. Because accreditation guidelines called for one counselor for every 400 or so students, a small school sought counselors for this sort of specialized function when much of it could be informally fulfilled by its teachers.

All of these factors had the effect of making it more difficult for teachers, students, and administrators to agree on a direction for the school simply because so many more people's views needed to be considered. To mollify disgruntled taxpayers, a superintendent might pronounce that all the district's schools offer a similar program and then set about homogenizing them to fit that pronouncement. The school's philosophy becomes someone else's platitude rather than being guided by the faculty.

In this regard, schools seem to be one step behind the industrial model they began emulating in the 1920s (Callahan 1962). In industry, the view of workers as machines escalated until the primacy of pride in one's work was replaced by a desire to simply make it through the day. In schools, the transformation has reached the point where teachers and students form unwritten pacts: "I won't try to make you learn anything if you won't cause any disruptions in my classroom." As a researcher for the Carnegie Commission's study of the high school put it:

> There are schools in this country where teachers will tell you that the most important technological innovation in use in the schools today is not the television or the computer, but the Sony Walkman. (Hout 1983)

This innocent piece of technology allows students, forced by law to be in school, to remove themselves psychologically from an unworkable situation. In turn, teachers can look over their quiet, docile classes and pretend that they are teaching.

Industry now is rapidly reconceptualizing the role of the worker, acknowledging the importance of community by creating small, independent work teams and quality circles — small discussion groups that give workers a forum for suggesting revisions in the production process. People issues were ignored until shoddy workmanship began to result in lost sales. Considering people's needs has become good business. Education is now due to take this next step; this transformation will occur more easily and naturally in small schools.

For the change to happen, all the key people must value community. Two examples of small high schools that "feel" like large high schools will illustrate the point. The first, a school in Colorado with about 150 students, has a principal who openly expresses the goal of making his school into a miniature comprehensive high school before he retires. He has many good ideas but governs with a firm hand. There are periodic insurrections by the staff, who hold a different image for the school, one that features a more informal, less rule-bound atmosphere in which learning could be conceptualized in many ways other than formally scheduled classes.

These two competing philosophies ebb and flow, giving the school a schizoid personality that is debilitating to students, the principal, and especially the teachers. Some teachers have tolerated the situation for many years because they value the role that the school, even with its constraints, allows them to play. But one comes away from a visit to the school with a strong sense of the opportunities lost. The Conant model strongly defines what is legitimate in this school, and the conflicts of philosophy and style it precipitates continually assault the school's sense of community.

A second school in Wyoming has accomplished the goal of becoming a miniature comprehensive high school. A staff of 21 delivers a three-track curriculum to 175 students. A high degree of specialization exists. Besides a principal, assistant principal, and full-time counselor, the school has two art teachers, two business teachers, a reading specialist, and a vocational education teacher. The comprehensive model is so faithfully installed that even the factions of teachers that typically exist in large high schools are present. Professionalism is defined by some teachers as doing their specialty with students and then sending them on to someone else. A prior principal, who sought to soften this compartmentalization of the curriculum (and of the child), was drummed out of the school by one faction of teachers. The current principal treads softly to avoid the same fate.

This school has a low teacher-student ratio, but the strongest bond between teachers and administrators seems to be the wary truce they share. The students, who attend the school by choice, seem satisfied though unexcited about its program; the climate compares quite favorably with what they had experienced in the community's large high schools. What might this school be if its teachers valued community as much as they do curriculum? What might it be if the confining concept of professionalism as specialization did not dominate the relationships of teachers to students and to colleagues? The remainder of this chapter will attempt to paint this picture.

What Small High Schools Do for Teachers

If a school does not work for teachers, it has little chance of working for students. But it is an increasingly difficult task to make large schools supportive environments for teachers. The number of teachers in a school becomes critical before the number of students does.

All the teachers in a school need to feel that they play an important role in setting its course. Therefore, the number of teachers in a school must be reduced to the point where all teachers can sit down and plan the course of the school *as a group*. Much of group dynamics research sets the maximum size of such work groups at about 12 persons, and even this number is considered an upper limit.

Size is important in a second respect. Small size allows schools to establish their own identity and philosophy. If teachers, students, and parents of similar philosophy come together and create a school, another important dimension of community — a commonly shared set of values — can develop.

Six important transformations of the teaching role can occur with a reduction in size and the establishment of commonly shared values:

1. Teachers (and students) gain a heightened sense of their own efficacy.
2. The principal can become a head teacher and, as a result, remove the authority barrier with the rest of the faculty.
3. A functional support system for teachers can develop.
4. A truly democratic governance model can evolve.
5. The primacy of control issues can come to an end.
6. Teachers (and students) can more easily identify with the school.

Each of these six transformations markedly increases teachers' sense of their own importance to the school, which in turn has an effect on the total social climate of the school.

A Heightened Sense of Efficacy. Teachers have many good ideas to which a large school's structure has difficulty responding. In a small high school the potential exists to transform teachers from workers implementing someone else's ideas into much more autonomous professionals. They can become policy makers.

The change that occurs in teachers' attitudes toward their jobs and their school when they are able to play a direct role in setting policy is quite apparent as one visits small high schools. In many schools of this size, teachers spend an extraordinary amount of time in staff meetings. We know of one high school of perhaps 150 students in Illinois that has a one- to two-hour staff meeting several afternoons each week. This is not a requirement of the job; it is simply seen by these teachers as the best way to run *their* school.

This sense of professional efficacy is critical to teachers' satisfaction. Lytle (1980) relates an incident that occurred in the Parkway Program, a small high school program established in Philadelphia in 1969 (Bremer and von Moschzisker 1971). Lytle likens teaching conditions at Parkway to those Lortie lists in his important sociological study, *Schoolteacher* (1975), as promoting teacher satisfaction. A court-ordered reassignment of teachers on the basis of race required the transfer of about 55% of Parkway's teachers, who were among the more than 1,000 Philadelphia teachers in the reassignment process. Lytle continues the story:

> [These teachers] were brought together in groups of 100 or more
> to bid in seniority order on positions in the 28 senior highs and

35 junior highs. The only information they were given before making this choice was school name, subject area, and "race" of position. Because they knew so little about the schools and had only a minute or two to make a choice, teachers tended to pick schools near their homes. (p. 701)

The teachers who selected Parkway had little idea of the kind of high school, actually five small high schools, in which they were electing to teach. They also entered the program at its nadir; the teacher/student ratio had risen markedly, and staff morale was very low.

Although they had to adapt almost immediately to a work situation different from any they had previously experienced, the newcomers assimilated quickly. They designed courses they'd never taught before, organized extracurricular activities, and got involved with every dimension of the school. (p. 701)

In February of that tumultuous year, a second reassignment plan allowed many of the uprooted teachers to return to their original schools *if* there were vacancies in their teaching area. Two groups of teachers — Parkway's original teachers who had been forced out and their new replacements — now had to choose between the two teaching settings they had experiened.

First option went to former Parkway teachers who had been laid off or reassigned to other schools. Every one of these teachers requested to return to Parkway, although all had options to take other positions. Fourteen met the racial and subject criteria and were actually able to return. Of the seven remaining vacancies, five were in subject areas that matched those of teachers assigned to Parkway the previous September. All five were filled by teachers who had originally been assigned to Parkway against their will but who now chose to remain. Of the remaining 11 teachers who had been assigned in September, all but one indicated in discussions with the principal that they would have preferred to remain at Parkway rather than going to another school. (p. 702)

The significance of these events is clear. Even in a large, bureaucratic school system like Philadelphia's, the combination of small size and a transformed school culture has much potency, even for understandably disgruntled teachers. Lytle laments,

we seem to have forgotten the importance of the teacher and his or her job satisfaction as prerequisites of effective schooling. It would seem obvious that youngsters aren't going to be taught well unless their teachers find this work satisfying. (p. 702)

Teachers in small high schools do pay a price. They are confronted with a much more complex role. The comfort and security that comes with the familiar isolation of teaching evaporates when a small staff operates cooperatively. They also work very hard. Things that "must be done" are regularly raised by the group, and these teachers know that they will be the chief doers. Because these burdens tend to be self-imposed, they are carried out, if not eagerly at least without the resistance and complaints that often characterize implementation efforts in large schools. For teachers with this level of involvement, "pitching in" happens naturally.

> *Item:* We attended a faculty meeting at a small school in Pennsylvania. The main agenda item was planning two parent-information nights designed to inform families, who were considering transferring to the school, about its program. The apparent best process would have all teachers at the school for two long evenings near the end of the school year. The proposal caught the staff drained of energy and pressed for time. After a long discussion, the staff, to a person, reluctantly accepted the plan as "the right thing to do."

In almost any large high school such a proposal probably would fail. It would be seized as an opportunity for the workers to stand up for their rights and defeat management's "unreasonable" proposal.

A New Role for the Principal. Administrators, too, are transformed by small high schools. Schools of the size we are talking about seldom need full-time administrators, even under circumstances in which a central administration has done little to ease the demands of the bureaucracy. A principal can be involved in at least one teaching experience a day and probably more. The "we-they" suspicions that teachers and administrators often harbor toward each other dissipate as their roles overlap. The role of the principal reverts to its historical roots before the title was truncated from the original "principal teacher."

Principal teachers or head teachers, the term we prefer, have an enhanced credibility with three key constituencies: their teachers, for reasons already discussed; their students, because head teachers see them on a day-to-day basis in relaxed situations rather than in the strained ones that typify visits to the principal's office; and the parents, because head teachers, with little opportunity to become isolated in the front office, have a more intimate view of the school and of their children.

In turn, head teachers lose credibility with two other important audiences: their administrative colleagues in other schools, with whom they have less in common in their new role; and their central administration superiors, who may become upset when the head teacher is unable to attend meetings because of teaching conflicts and may question whether these people should be receiving a principal's salary rather than a teacher's.

A Support System. People will establish workable size units whether the organization in which they work facilitates it or not. Whether these groups are called cliques or factions or departments, they serve two functions: They make living in the organization more satisfying, and they set boundaries that keep people from building identification with the large organization. These sorts of tensions are largely absent in small settings.

Large high schools sometimes succeed in building a feeling of belonging to a group of workable size by encouraging strong, clearly defined academic departments, each housed in its own identifiable section of the building. To the extent that this effort succeeds, it inadvertently works against the equally important identification of individuals with the whole faculty. Specialization and confining one's involvement with students within a set of well-defined boundaries are implicit in the arrangement.

Small high schools do not exact this sort of compromise. Teachers in them do not trade strong relationships with a few for anonymity with many others. However, these schools do pay a price. Because a small staff must be stretched to offer a complete curriculum, specialists are rare. Teachers may teach in several areas, including some in which their expertise is quite thin. In some ways, the program may suffer; Conant, and any other observer who ascribes to the teacher-as-expert concept, would likely be appalled by the situation. But as Horwood points out, something can be added to teaching in such situations:

> All of the students commented that the teachers were "knowledgeable." Some informants gave examples of teacher knowledge that impressed them. In one case, a teacher known for prowess in higher mathematics gave a course on the Viet Nam war in cooperation with a Social Studies teacher. In other cases, similar crossing of subject boundaries or the development of innovative courses to match particular student interests were cited as examples of admirable teacher competence. A number of students were also sensitive to the paradox that, in their eyes, a teacher's knowledge was sometimes displayed in comfortable admissions of ignorance.

> The younger students were impressed that the teachers were willing to learn new things, to try new tasks, to display precisely the joy in learning expected of the students. They interpreted this quality of the teachers as a highly valued sign of strength and confidence. (Horwood 1983, pp. 62-63)

Teachers who succeed, even excel, under these informal conditions often share two traits. They enjoy diversity and are truly generalists, who value the commonalities across disciplines rather than emphasize the differences between them. And they have largely abandoned the teaching model most linked with expert teachers, the lecture.

Governance. Teachers with a role in governance are much more likely to see value in sharing that power with their students.

> The teachers claimed to like the school better than their previous schools because they had a say in policies and events. They felt that they had some power. Students also felt that they [the students] had some power, because, as they pointed out and as I saw for myself, the program was continually being fine-tuned with their participation through the mechanism of Governance. Similarly, the representation of students on all administrative committees, like a hiring committee, convinced them that they contributed to the shape of life at the school. (Horwood 1983, p. 88)

In small, less complex high schools, trusting students carries much less risk than it does in large high schools. As a result, small high schools of the sort we are describing often develop governance models notable for their diversity but with the laudable purpose of involving students in activities that more directly prepare one to be a responsible citizen in today's complex society.

Students (and teachers) do not always respond productively to unbridled democracy. Sharing power is a delicate business. Any school that one day gives students no power and the next gives them true equality courts anarchy. Schools that make the change gradually as students (and teachers) are ready for it, pursue a wise course. The point is to aspire to the goal and steadily progress toward it.

The superficiality of the large high school's student council pales in comparison with the practices that are possible in small high schools.

> *Item:* A small, autonomous program inside a huge high school in Indiana runs a weekly town meeting. A different senior presides at each meeting. School policies, disciplinary actions to be taken for particular transgressions, and the future direction of the program are typical agenda items. Teachers and students all have one vote in the deliberation process.

Again, schools do not make a change like this all at once. It evolves incrementally. But once small trusts in students are rewarded, the door is open to larger advances requiring greater risks. Teacher autonomy (power) is helpful to students. It strengthens the power and autonomy allowed students. Autonomy begets autonomy. "We-they" suspicions begin to dissipate as teachers and students share power. As a first-year student in a small high school put it:

> The traditional school is strong on control. The teachers are there controlling the kids. Locks on the doors. Then what they did here was they took out the control and gave us trust. And it seems to work a lot better because you have to motivate yourself. (Horwood 1983, pp. 51-52)

But teachers in high schools run in this way must live with the gnawing question, "Will this be the time they fail the trust?"

Minimizing Control Responsibilities. Large high schools must maintain control, and the primary agent for doing so is the teacher. Closing a campus at lunch time has an impact on student freedom and autonomy; but what is less often considered is its impact on teachers, who must enforce the confinement. Students' resentment of the situation is directed, quite naturally, at their teacher-keepers. Student-teacher relationships erode. Teachers are distracted from their primary role; human energy is sapped by these control responsibilities; and a noble profession is made petty.

A small high school can substitute internalized forms of control for the more typical control measures such as a long list of rules and prescribed penalties for infractions.

> The informants were impressed that the school had only three rules, all of them prohibitive and very simple: No drinking; no drugs; no sex. The students experienced a strong sense of independence from these simple and apparently reasonable restraints. It is interesting that they did not see the restriction of smoking to the smoking porch, nor the limited hours of coffee and snack service in Munchie as "rules." Here was evidence of the absence of imposition and assumption of responsibility. (Horwood 1983, p. 56)

The significance of the reduced level of control possible in small high schools is not the freedom it gives students but the freedom it gives teachers. It permits them to concentrate on teaching; and by eliminating major points of conflict between students and teachers, it offers more opportunities to build strong, supportive relationships. Horwood's (1983) observation is again pertinent:

69

I had some difficulty in uncovering what a "discipline problem" would look like in the school. The reason for the difficulty was not a reluctance to talk about it but an almost total lack of opportunity for breaches of discipline in the sense usually understood in schools. The students were highly conscious of the absence of compulsion in the program while recognizing its generally demanding nature. The absence of a large number of rules and regulations was identified as helping to keep teachers from being perceived as enforcers of school law and order. (p. 64)

Identification with the School. Teachers in a small high school naturally develop a strong identity with it. As a pregnant teacher, anticipating her departure from teaching in a small school in Colorado, told us,

Here I am, with a coveted position in what may be the best school in the country, about to give it up with little hope of ever getting back in it. It hurts. It hurts like hell!

Under such circumstances, teachers bring unusual levels of support to a program. When it is troubled, they are troubled. When it triumphs, they triumph.

The students ... were convinced that the teachers enjoyed their work, that they liked being at the school. For several students, this was in sharp contrast to previous experience where "teachers didn't seem to like their jobs and they certainly didn't like you." (Horwood 1983, p. 63)

A high level of identification with a program makes teaching an attractive profession for many who choose to enter it. Teaching must include large doses of such tonic for teachers to thrive.

What Small High Schools Do for Students

The number of students becomes critical when it exceeds the number that most of the professional staff can know by name; anonymity works against everything for which a school strives. Barker and Gump (1964), who studied small comprehensive high schools, defined maximum size in terms of student participation:

Our findings and our theory posit a negative relationship between school size and individual student participation. What seems to happen is that as schools get larger and settings inevitably become more heavily populated, more of the students are less needed; they become superfluous, redundant.

What size should a school be?

The data of this research and our own educational values tell us that a school should be sufficiently small that all of its students

70

are needed for its enterprises. A school should be small enough
that students are not redundant. (p. 202)

Students in a small high school experience an enlivened curriculum
that encourages their full involvement, a program of offerings that can
be tailored to each individual, the emergence of greater self-confidence
in one's own decisions, and an increasingly more positive attitude toward school. Five transformations in student relationships that small
schools permit are of particular interest:

1. They encourage expansion of the students' roles.
2. They heighten students' sense of responsibility and accountability.
3. They stimulate a collegiality between students and teachers.
4. They increase students' access to adults.
5. They develop a sense of belonging to a community.

Expansion of the Student's Role. Large high schools give students
a preset agenda of course offerings and who will offer them. Students
acquiesce to this prescribed plan. They learn quickly that their ideas
are not important in the curriculum building process. Adults are there
to design the curriculum *for* young people, and in the final analysis,
it is the adults' school, not the students'. Also, an individual student's
ideas of what is good for him or her are considered only as long as
they can be met *within* the established curriculum. Students whose
needs are not met through the curriculum may be viewed as a worri-
some complication. If they or their parents assert their rights to an
appropriate education, they may be viewed as troublemakers who are
complicating an already complex enterprise.

Most large high schools expect students to function in a relatively
narrow role. Students can *respond* to the program, but they cannot
initiate it. Opportunities for an expanded role are usually limited to
informal, extracurricular activities — activities that many adults state
were their most significant learning experiences (Flanagan 1978). Ironically, the reform reports recommend reducing the important role these
informal activities now play in large high schools.

Small schools can bring this informality into the curriculum quite
easily. The resources of a small staff are limited, so offering a complete program requires one to consider ways of learning beyond the
typical classroom model of one teacher working with a group of students for five periods a week. Students are a resource for making the
program whole. Parts of the program may become independent learning activities. Students and their teachers look to the community for

volunteers with expertise to supplement ongoing activities. These volunteers, often people who enjoy teaching but who have chosen to pursue more lucrative careers, sometimes teach entire courses. In some small high schools, students themselves sometimes teach classes. When students are asked to play roles that an adult normally would play in a large school, new opportunities for growth are provided.

Heightened Sense of Responsibility. In small high schools it is easier to implement activities that encourage students to take on more responsibility. This becomes important when a small number of professionals has to play such a wide variety of roles. Students in a small high school are known to their teachers. Teachers are aware of what levels of responsibility students can handle. But small size alone is insufficient; many small high schools do little more to expand student responsibility than do large high schools. The point is that they have more potential to do so successfully if they so choose.

Collegiality with Teachers and Access to Adults. As the student's role expands, it does so primarily in the direction of the teacher's role. In other words, the respective responsibilities of teachers and students begin to merge. Students find that they are doing things *with* teachers rather than *for* teachers.

> Andy and Juanita both revealed the older students' tendency to accept responsibility beyond their own immediate concerns. For Andy, it was expressed as an obvious requirement that he help new students to "catch on" by being helpful to the teachers. Juanita more precisely identified the same idea in terms of a role model and illustrated it specifically in her participation as a student aide in Beginnings and Learning to Learn [two orientation classes for entering students]. "You develop obligations to classes and to main functions and being part of the school. The school demands a little bit more of you in being a ... role model." (Horwood 1983, p. 52)

As students take on more responsibility in directing their learning and as they build confidence in their capabilities, an important form of collegiality with teachers can begin to develop (Benne 1970). The sort of identification with the school that is fostered for teachers extends to students. As students make their mark on the program, it increasingly becomes their school. The pitching-in phenomenon can begin to affect them as well as their teachers. The seeds of collegiality are planted.

A major problem for teachers or students in any school is finding time to talk informally to each other. When a school is structured to fill every minute of the day, it eliminates most of the possibilities for students and teachers to "just talk." Adolescents need adult confidants beyond their parents. Before families became so mobile, aunts, uncles, and older cousins often filled this role. Sensing this need, the administration of a large high school in an Eastern state sought to build time into the schedule for such informal interchanges. Teachers would offer "high interest" classes or just be available to students for individual help. When we visited the school, the plan was failing. Teachers resented the time reductions in other classes to make room for this new activity, and they saw it as an additional preparation. Students viewed it in a variety of ways, but a majority simply used the time as an additional study hall.

One might conclude from the experiment that it was trying to fill an imaginary need. We suspect the plan was failing primarily because it attempted to schedule formally what must be an informal, spontaneous activity. Installing informal activities in bureaucratic settings is almost always a force fit.

When the daily schedule of a school is relaxed, time for spontaneous discussions begins to appear. Some small high schools have adopted a scheduling format where teachers and students both have large blocks of free time. The risks associated with granting such a level of freedom in large settings are many. But the plan works quite well in a number of small high schools. In Chapter 6, we shall examine closely the program of one such small high school in Colorado.

During "free" time, students have the opportunity to engage in adultlike conversations with teachers; in other words, they can *practice* being adults. Teachers, in turn, have this time to decompress from the high levels of energy and concentration that teaching entails. And both teachers and students have the opportunity to really get to know each other as people. The gains for students in such programs are not measured in SAT scores or achievement test percentiles. They are measured in steps toward maturity.

A Feeling of Belonging. Some students in a high school, regardless of its size, come to identify strongly with it, to care about it. They invest considerable energy in making it work better. They engage in many different activities, often becoming leaders. They represent the 15% of the student body that William Glasser (1976) labels "winners." He makes the point that, no matter how good or how bad the school, about 15% of the students will carry this appellation. They thrive on the attention. They feel they are part of the school. They belong. Their teachers are gratified by their involvement and achievement. More importantly, they are a continuing reassurance that the school still works because a young person is willing to invest energy in it.

But what of the other 85%? Glasser says they are, in one way or another, "losing." We can speculate on some of the reasons. First the parental support on which schools have depended for generations is no longer there. Schools and especially teachers increasingly find themselves taking on parenting functions, a demanding task under any circumstances but a terribly difficult one in a large high school. In contrast, small high schools possess considerable potential for helping youths with such needs. In his interviews with students in a small high school, Horwood (1983) continually encountered comments that centered on the concept encapsulated in the cliché, "one big happy family":

> [T]he idea was articulated in several ways. Andy said, "We're a team here." Lucille's words were, "Everybody's really close, not just some people." And Marie assured me that, "Here you feel like you're at home." As I learned more about the backgrounds of the students and the significant number from broken families, it seemed to me that their references to family-like relationships expressed the filling of a great need. (pp. 61-62)

In affluent suburbia such surrogate parenting may entail providing psychic support or just talking an issue through. In economically depressed areas it also may include providing food and clothing, occasionally even shelter. Some youths need little of this attention; some need much more than the school, no matter how ideal, can reasonably supply.

The control pressures and scheduling constraints in large high schools make this sort of individual attention impractical. The steady procession of group after group of students through a teacher's classroom through the segmented school day takes on the accouterments of the assembly line. Even caring teachers must dole out individual attention in one- or two-minute packets at the beginning and end of classes. Students with "mild cases" tend to hide their problems, while severe cases are shunted off to one or another specialist.

Through it all, many teachers rightly feel harried and ineffective, and many students rightly feel abandoned. Only with extraordinary effort can the structure of the large high school accommodate these needs. When the high school was designed three generations ago, students with such needs seldom entered high school. If they did, they were expected to fall in step or drop out.

Society's expectations for the high school have changed dramatically in the intervening decades, but the high school's original structure

74

remains essentially intact. The mechanism is strained to the point of environmental collapse, a circumstance in which people simply withdraw, first psychologically and then physically, from a social system that no longer meets their needs. The situation was considered serious in the 1960s when alarming numbers of capable students were dropping out. It is now considered a crisis because teachers are joining them.

When a school is small enough that scheduling is not primarily a control mechanism, it can permit the free time that teachers and students need just to talk. Such informality offers the potential for successfully dealing with all but the most severe needs of youth. Teachers begin to feel productive because they are solving the problems that need to be solved rather than ignoring all but those that can be solved in one- and two-minute sessions. Equally important, almost all students can experience a reasonable amount of attention. They can begin to reciprocate by getting more involved in the school community rather than withdrawing from it. They can, once again, belong.

The Case for Small High Schools

The strength of our convictions about the "rightness" of small high schools stems from our decade of work in large and, especially, small high schools (ones that have consciously built school cultures very different from the prevailing industrial model). That they can work so well at so many levels surprises us. That they seem so natural a way to keep school in today's society impresses us. That they lead to relaxed relationships between adults and youth pleases us. That they are fundamentally so sensible convinces us.

Despite these accumulating experiences over the years, an inner voice told us such purposefully small schools would always be a minority in the larger educational context. The tradeoffs would be too great for the majority. The rites and rituals of the large high school — the Friday night game, the honors classes, the college-type physical facilities, and the Prom — were too integral a part of the social fabric to be dislodged in our lifetimes.

Of the many events that have changed that view, two stand out: First, the accelerating mood of crisis suggests that the public high school must change or risk replacement by some other agency, most likely private education. The large public high school is in jeopardy of environmental collapse. Second, we have learned that what we thought were inevitable program limitations in small, informal schools with small teaching staffs and limited facilities do not have to occur. Indeed, we are increasingly convinced that small, supportive environments, which we have always thought to be superior at meeting the social and psychological needs of youth, have the potential for also delivering not just an equivalent but even a superior academic program at no additional cost. Horwood (1983) found among his student informants strong support of this idea:

> The students agreed that [their high school] ... offered more than did other schools. This perception was in striking contrast to the smallness of the school and the apparently limited ability of the staff to mount a large diversity of courses and workshops. But the students did not see the school's offerings as being limited to the intra-mural curriculum. Debra told me, "Anything is possible here. I can go to Australia ... I can learn to ... fly a plane. I can do virtually anything I want provided I put the effort into it." Marie put it that the school, "... gives you opportunities to explore." ... and Andy, more picturesquely, expressed the thought as, "It's a perfect place to live out your fantasies in education. You find out what you want to do and go out there and do it." (pp. 69-70)

Much of this book is our attempt to convey the set of experiences we have had in high schools of varying size that have led us not only to *feel* that small high schools are right — an untenable position for researchers — but to conclude that they *are* right from the accumulating evidence.

Chapter 5
Why Not Change Large High Schools?

*Strong cultures are not only able to respond to an environ-
ment, but they also adapt to diverse and changing circumstances. When times are tough, these companies can reach
deeply into their shared values and beliefs for the truth and courage to see them through. When new challenges arise, they can
adjust. This is exactly what companies are going to have to
do as we begin to experience a revolution in the structure of
modern organizations.*

> — Terrence Deal and Allan Kennedy
> (1982, pp. 195-96)

We can easily substitute *schools* for *companies* in the above quota-
tion to indicate the "revolution in the structure" of high schools that
is needed. If we simply could convert all high schools to what we have
argued is a reasonable size, say 250 students or less, there would be
no need for any other change strategy. While small size alone is not
sufficient, it opens up the possibilities for significant change.

Many communities, especially those with only one high school, will
not abandon their large high schools. Such high schools are often the
center of community life. Large segments of a community may turn
out for band concerts and school plays. The entire town shows up for
the Saturday night game, the outcome of which may take on mythic
proportions.

Item: Unlike most states, Indiana does not divide its state basketball tournament into several classes; the smallest high school competes against the largest. Almost every year finds a very small high school achieving the "Sweet Sixteen." In 1985, it was little Austin's (pop. 5,000) turn. For some residents, it was the event of a lifetime. The police chief yielded to a public head-shaving; a wedding ceremony was rescheduled to coincide with the half-time of one game. A team member wondered at the community support: "We can feel it," he said. "We can see it in their faces; how bad and how much they want it, too. It makes us play harder." A former coach, now administrator, added, "The fans seem to play the game with the kids. It's a family-type situation." The regional championship was capped by a siren-blowing parade and party attended by an estimated 2,000 of the town's residents that lasted until 1:00 a.m. . . .

According to Tom Sexton, who teaches chemistry and biology at the high school, "There has never been anything that has united the community like this." (*Louisville Courier-Journal*, 12 March 1985, pp. D1-D5)

Accepting that high schools often are far more than just places of learning, what can be done to change them? What can be done to bring to the classroom the levels of commitment and involvement that are devoted to extracurricular activities? The first, somewhat facetious answer that comes to mind is nothing. The evidence accumulated over the years from many reform efforts shows that large high schools do not change in any significant way, no matter what one does to them. They did not change during the heyday of the Progressive Education Movement in the 1920s and 1930s. They did not change following the Sputnik-inspired curriculum reforms of the 1960s. They did not change under the Education Professions Development Act during the 1960s and early 1970s. They did not change much as a result of the alternative-schools movement of that same period. And they probably will not change that much in the 1980s and beyond. But high schools, even large ones, can be different; there is much evidence to support such a statement (see for example, Rutter et al. 1979). If the high school is to survive, a number of characteristics of the large high school will have to change.

What kind of change is needed? We do not pretend to have a cookbook answer to this question that will apply to all high schools. Rather, we shall suggest some basic directions and guiding principles for changing the large high school, as well as some specifics on where to begin and how to proceed.

78

Three Levels of Change

Large high schools need to change at three levels: 1) the technical, 2) the managerial, and 3) the cultural. Past reform efforts have made the mistake of concentrating on one level, usually the technical, to the exclusion of the other two. Of course, the introduction of an innovation at any level is no guarantee that any significant change is taking place. One must look to what is happening as a result of the change. Conflict is one indicator that can be used to gauge the extent of the change; that is, the greater the conflict the more likely extensive change is taking place.

1. *Technical Change.* Technical change is designed to strengthen and refine the efforts of those who implement the present system of schooling. In other words, people will do something new or do an existing task more effectively. The targets for technical change are the individual teachers and paraprofessionals who carry out the current system of schooling. Technical changes might include the introduction of new technology (overhead projectors and computers), new ways of organizing for instruction (homogeneous grouping, continuous progress, team-teaching), and new curricula (sex education and computer literacy). Other technical changes involve personnel, for example, adding paraprofessionals or inservice programs for teachers.

Most of the changes that have been brought about in high schools through several reform periods have been technical changes. The host of new curricular programs triggered by Sputnik were aimed initially at revitalizing mathematics and science. Eventually, other areas of the curriculum, particularly English, social studies, and foreign languages, were included. These new curricula, designed not by educators but by professors in the various disciplines, were introduced to teachers through summer institutes at colleges and universities. After examining the content of federal legislation in education, Smith (1972) concluded that most of it entailed technical change.

Technical changes may have implications for the managerial and cultural levels; but more typically, they represent relatively simple, straightforward changes that substitute one set of materials or techniques for an existing set of materials or techniques.

Technical changes fit into existing patterns of schooling. They are as much shaped by the system as they shape the system. As long as we view schooling as teacher action and student reception, no amount of technical change will alter that fundamental practice.

These changes do not challenge the basic goals of the institution or the way in which it is structured. They assume that schools will continue to function much as they have in the past. While individual teachers may be threatened by and resist such changes, the school as a system is not threatened by them.

Technical change can be potent. For example, introducing large numbers of computers into the schools could have far-reaching effects on the entire culture of the schools. They could change teachers' roles, the way in which instruction is carried out, the way in which students and teachers interact, and the way in which the school is managed. Change at the technical level can have an impact at the other levels, but many forces resist this possibility. The introduction of new technology usually is made to conform to the existing structures of a school.

2. *Managerial Change*. Managerial change is designed to broaden, expand, and open up the system. If successful, the system becomes more responsive to the needs of a wider range of people. Managerial change results in changes in the distribution of power and authority, in new patterns of participation in decision making, and in increased monitoring of decisions by persons outside the formal authority structures.

Because such changes focus on issues of power, control, governance, authority, and decision making, they affect the managers of the school system: department heads, building principals, assistant principals, and central office administrators. Change at this level is likely to promote greater participation in school decisions by teachers, students, parents, and other members of the community. Examples of such change include the establishment of neighborhood school boards and school advisory councils and giving students the same power as teachers and administrators in making school decisions.

In part, the Ocean Hill-Brownsville controversy in the 1960s was due to a managerial change. Briefly, Ocean Hill-Brownsville was one of 30 local governing boards established by the New York City School Board to decentralize policy making in that mammoth school system. When several teachers that the Ocean Hill-Brownsville Board deemed incompetent were summarily fired, the teachers for the entire city went out on strike. The price of their return was the emasculation of the local boards' powers. The managerial change that had been implemented was more than the teachers could tolerate.

Another example of managerial change was the Education Professions Development Act enacted during the 1960s. One of its purposes was to create a dialogue between several of the stakeholder groups that were interested in improving education. Some of the meetings with low-income parents became quite stormy. The parents directed their anger and frustration at educators for not doing a better job because their children were not learning. Often these groups, aided and abetted by teachers who were in sympathy with them, struggled with principals for control of "their schools."

3. *Cultural Change.* Cultural change is the most significant kind of change because it often results in upheaval of the system. Cultural change results in a new set of instructional values, new patterns of relationships between students and teachers, new understandings of the nature of schooling, and new myths and symbols appropriate to the new culture. Since each person within the school is a carrier of the symbols and belief structures of schooling, all are targets of a cultural change.

Changes in the culture of a school are rightly perceived as a threat to the entire system of schooling. Such changes either call into question or actually require the replacement of the present culture with another, quite different culture. In calling for a "deschooling" of society, Ivan Illich (1970) was advocating a major cultural change.

A change at the cultural level may affect the technical and managerial levels, but its impact may not be clearly visible. For example, instruction may seem to go on as it has in the past, but it is governed by a new set of values. More often, however, a cultural change is so fundamental that it is reflected in both new instructional practices and management procedures.

One outcome of developing a strong sense of community within high schools is that the very act of doing so stimulates cultural change. The culture of large high schools is governed by one basic value, order, and its ancillary values, silence and passivity, values that pervade the entire system of schooling. A new-found sense of community changes all that. There is increased communication between all of the stakeholders in the school. Teachers have to talk to students, who in turn have to talk to each other; all of them have to talk to the principal. Another outcome of a strong sense of community is the commitment it generates in the people involved; commitment leads inevitably to action. Students and teachers in a strong community are more eager to engage one another actively. Finally, community leads to increased participation, which in turn creates a new sense of order derived from the needs of both the individuals and the group as a whole.

Bringing about cultural change in large high schools is a formidable task. The size and complexity of the large comprehensive high school works against the development of the consensus on which cultural change must rest. This is not to say that there are no prospects for change, but only to emphasize the difficulty in bringing it about.

Principles for Changing Schools

Educational reform, if it is to be successful, must be aimed first at the culture of the school. Technical and managerial change will follow as they are needed to fit the new culture. Building a strong sense of community creates the medium in which cultural change can occur and opens the way for further change.

As a framework for discussing change in large high schools, we shall use eight basic principles identified by Peters and Waterman (1982) in their study of successful corporations. While we recognize that it may not be appropriate to use industry as a model for changing schools, we do so without apology because so many of the business concepts implied by such terms as accountability, efficiency, and management-by-objectives have been thoroughly incorporated into the educational literature. There is no little irony in that large high schools, over the past half century, have emulated big business to the point where only solutions that have proved themselves in big business settings seem viable for large high schools.

Peters and Waterman, if they do nothing else, place the emphasis where it belongs: on people, their willingness to change, their openness to change and, under the right conditions, their eagerness to change. One thing the best corporations have in common is a belief that people make the difference. Teachers and administrators need to start acting as though they also make a difference. It has been difficult for them to do so in the last few years with all the criticism that has been hurled at them. But believing in themselves again is a good place to begin.

Interestingly, while Peters and Waterman make no reference to a sense of community, many of the practices in the best corporations seem to stem from that idea. They speak about corporations being rigid with respect to their core values, just as schools are. A key difference between corporations and schools is that the pressures of the marketplace force corporations to make their values congruent with their goals. Peters and Waterman also speak of the many ways that corporations reinforce their values. If employees accept the core values, they often are free to challenge even the basic technology of the corporation.

82

In *In Search of Excellence*, Peters and Waterman point out that some businesses are very successful, others are not. Eight principles seem to account for most of these differences:

- a bias for action;
- stay close to the customer;
- autonomy and entrepreneurship;
- productivity through people;
- hands-on, value-driven activity;
- stick to the knitting;
- simple form, lean staff; and
- simultaneous loose-tight properties.

Many of the most successful corporations go to great lengths to create working environments that encourage and reward people for doing their best. These environments are sorely needed at the high school level. As many of the reform reports have suggested, we desperately need schools that work *for* teachers and *for* students. If big business can change in order to be successful, large high schools can do the same. But it will not be easy. Peters and Waterman's eight principles suggest a direction.

A Bias for Action. Everyone knows of the inertia inherent in large organizations. To get things started, much less accomplished, requires a great deal of effort, most of it spent in getting past the requirements of data collection and analysis, studies, and internal reports. Planning is important; but it should not impede action, especially in a period of rapid change. Action needs to be taken to deal with problems. People who are closest to the problem, who are most familiar with it, are expected to take the action. In the best corporations, people will be criticized more for not taking action than for making the wrong move.

High schools, more than most institutions, need a bias for action. Most of them are so mired in curriculum guides, rules and regulations, standardized instructional routines, and a heavily scheduled day that little thought is given to solving problems. And because teachers are given so little autonomy, they tend not to identify and address problems.

At the district level, a bias for action would place more accountability in the hands of individual schools. This would allow for differences in individual and instructional styles and personalities and permit action to be taken by those close to where the problems and opportunities arise. Small, autonomous schools have a distinct advantage in developing a bias for action.

Item: A small high school in Colorado responded quickly to news of an impending solar eclipse by planning a trip to Montana, the closest location from where the total eclipse could be viewed. The trip went off successfully. But what if it had been cloudy in Montana that day? These teachers' bias for action was so strong that they had not considered the possibility!

We are told that the Montana city they visited has two large high schools of its own. How their students reportedly spent the afternoon of the eclipse says much about the impact of size. Both schools apparently feared liability should students burn their retinas while viewing the eclipse without proper equipment. One school responded by ushering all of its students into the auditorium and showing them movies during the critical period. The other simply gave its students the afternoon off; if they were to watch the eclipse, they could burn their retinas on their own time. Probably, most of the students in this Montana town who did experience this once-in-a-lifetime event were from that small high school in Colorado.

A bias for action also implies greater control over the necessary resources. Deciding quickly to travel to Montana to view an eclipse and having the funds to do so are two different issues. If complete budgets were allocated to each building with flexibility as to how funds were spent, there would be real differences in how individual schools function. Not all high schools in the same town would have to look alike. Each could have distinctive programs in which it chose to invest disproportionate resources.

Stay Close to the Customer. The most successful businesses are in close touch with their customers. They know their customers' wants and needs, and they make every effort to respond.

High schools seldom pay much attention to their "customers." If the customers are unsatisfied, it is because they are too immature, too lacking in judgment, or too uncooperative. A recent study of teacher evaluation practices in southern Indiana schools (Smith, Walden, and Weaver 1986) indicates that high school teachers reject student evaluations because they believe that students are not able to judge good teaching. If staying in close touch with the customer were one of the guiding values of these high schools, teachers would not reject student evaluations out-of-hand; they would avidly seek them.

Many of the high school's customers simply are not buying what is being produced and sold. The number-one problem of schools, as judged by students, is not alcohol, discipline, or drugs, but apathy and boredom (McQuigg and Smith 1985). That many of the reform reports advocate more time-on-task, when the present tasks produce such over-whelming boredom, is the essence of irony.

Teachers often view being responsive to students as giving in to them. They fear a diminution of standards and a loss of control. Despite their reluctance to work *with* students, Sizer (1984) emphasizes that teachers invariably establish some form of social contract with them:

> Agreements in classrooms are never quite alike. They are negotiated by each teacher and class, with the concessions on each part being over the distance between the students' pleasure and level of awareness of a subject and the teacher's sense of their need and the imperatives of that subject. (p. 160)

Unfortunately, some teachers see little room for negotiation; they *know* what the customer needs.

In contrast, good teachers understand intuitively that they must consider students' interests and ideas, however whimsical they may appear to be. Each teacher must build on the ideas and experiences that students bring with them. By ignoring student ideas, teachers shut themselves off from student dialogue.

Students and teachers need personal contact over long periods of time, contact that arouses interest and involvement.

> *Item:* A teacher told us about encountering some of her students on a voluntary work crew during a flood. They were surprised to see each other there, filling, passing, and stacking sandbags to hold back the river that threatened their community. They worked side-by-side for many hours until darkness fell and the teacher became weary. Still, she marveled at the staying power of her students. They did not quit, nor did they seem to get tired. She noticed one boy telling others where to pile the bags to contain the river. She had never thought of him as a leader in her class; but she soon realized that in this setting he knew more, perhaps intuitively, than many of the adults.

After the rain-swollen river had subsided and they were back in the classroom, the teacher and these students were closer; they had been allies; they had a bond that had brought them together. This experience served as a bridge for other things they did in the classroom.

Personal contact allows teachers and students to experience each other's humanity. This was brought home by one of our students:

> I remember walking into a grocery store when I was in about seventh grade and seeing my teacher. I was appalled — I mean, my God, there she stood before me with slacks on (not her teaching

outfit) buying food. Until that time I just never considered that she ate.... I thought she survived on chalk dust or something. Anyway, that was my first realization that we were both humans and such a barrier between us really should not exist. (Gregory 1972, p. 111)

Certainly teachers cannot accept students' ideas unquestioningly. But neither can they ignore the most important person in the educational process — the student being educated. If more teachers adopted the "stay-close-to-the-customer" principle, we would have a drastically different culture in high schools.

Autonomy and Entrepreneurship. Peters and Waterman describe autonomy and entrepreneurship as breaking the corporation into small companies and encouraging them to think independently and competitively. Many of the reform reports of the 1970s made similar suggestions for schools. Break the large schools down, they said, and give more autonomy to small groups of teachers. Such a change forces people out of familiar routines; they have to think again about what they are doing. An air of excitement and adventure is created in which anything can happen. New possibilities and prospects become evident.

Schools need to develop a more lively spirit, a sense of adventure for both students and teachers. Without significant opportunities to make decisions and to sense their control over such decisions, students and teachers continually will be looking to someone else to guide their actions and activities. Teachers must learn to rely on their own instincts for classroom decisions; they must make many on-the-spot decisions in classrooms without benefit of previous discussion. Their students require opportunities for decision making that are not much different in character from those of the teacher. In this sense, shared decision making helps both groups to experience greater autonomy.

Few teachers or students think of themselves as entrepreneurs; yet much might be gained by their doing so. Above all else, entrepreneurs are risk-takers. They seek out new opportunities to display their talents and are willing to experiment with new methods and markets (clients). School districts would do well to establish incentives that make risk-taking more attractive to teachers and principals.

Some school districts, for example, are experimenting with new methods of distributing merit pay. Instead of giving such increments only to individual teachers, they are awarding some or all of the money to entire schools. Other districts are giving additional resources for materials, field trips, and other instructional purposes to schools that use their current resources to the fullest. If more of these resources were awarded to schools that are willing to take risks and experiment, entrepreneurship would be encouraged.

Productivity Through People. The idea of productivity through people, if properly introduced in school districts, would return the teacher and the student to their central place in schooling. While excellent materials are certainly important, they are not nearly as critical as a teacher who is committed, caring, and challenging. Peters and Waterman emphasize that people must be trusted as the responsible persons most of them are:

> Treat people as adults. Treat them as partners; treat them with dignity; treat them with respect. Treat *them* — not capital spending and automation — as the primary source of productivity gains. (p. 238)

Applied to schools, their concept holds the promise of freeing teachers from some of the bureaucratic busywork that some principals use to maintain personal control over everything that goes on in their school.

Peters and Waterman (p. 250) describe an innovation at Dana Corporation, a $3 billion-a-year maker of brass propeller blades and gearboxes. Dana did away with time clocks. At first the supervisors complained, "What do we do without time clocks?" Dana's president responded, "How do you manage any ten people? If you see them come in late regularly, you talk to them. Why do you need time clocks to know if the people who work for you are coming in late?" The anecdote's pertinence to schools and teachers may not seem readily apparent, but teachers' time is heavily controlled. All teachers on a faculty are required to remain in school all day when fewer could manage the school at certain times — during lunch, for example. In some districts, teachers *are* required to punch in and out each day. Are teachers really so untrustworthy that they require time clocks? Why not deal directly with the few who cannot get to school on time or who leave too early? Or is it that the schools these teachers work in are so large and impersonal that personal confrontation has become an alien concept?

Then there are the bells. Would that much time be lost if they never rang again? Students and teachers know what time each class starts and finishes. By trusting in both students and teachers, schools can emulate the direction of many excellent American corporations. We learned the lesson of efficiency from the business world when it was of dubious value to schools. Can we learn the lesson of trust from them when it is of critical importance?

Hands-On, Value-Driven Activity. If education has lost anything over the years, it is that overriding sense that the young will mature into decent, responsible human beings. It takes a certain amount of faith in the young to believe that maturation will occur, given enough time and support. Without this faith, education becomes lost in a tangle of test scores, behavior codes, accountability measures, and time-on-task ratings. There is nothing inherently wrong with such educational trappings, except the degree to which they represent activity without a guiding set of *shared* values.

A sense of community and common purpose is driven by commonly shared values. Thomas Watson, Jr., President of IBM, wrote:

> Consider any great organization — one that has lasted over the years — I think you will find that it owes its resiliency not to its form of organization or administrative skills, but to the power of what we call beliefs and the appeal these beliefs have for its people.... In other words, the basic philosophy, spirit and drive of an organization have far more to do with its relative achievements than do technological or economic resources, organizational structure, innovation, and timing. (Peters and Waterman 1982, p. 347)

This is unfamiliar language for a businessman. In business, we have learned, the bottom line is profit and survival. But according to Peters and Waterman, excellent corporations are driven by other motives, usually a set of beliefs and values that are shared widely throughout all levels of the corporation.

One of the features of small schools, difficult if not impossible to duplicate in large ones, is the belief in a core set of values that is shared by students and teachers alike. A large school must accommodate a wide variety of students and teachers, making consensus on primary values extraordinarily difficult to achieve. To the extent that values are articulated at all, they are over-generalized and over-idealized. Platitudes are never clearly linked to practice. Only when these values are realized in educational practice do fundamental disagreements become apparent. For example, many schools believe in self-discipline until it is translated into policies that permit students to make decisions — and mistakes.

As Peters and Waterman suggest, values are not usually transmitted through formal structures and procedures; they are "diffused by softer means: specifically [through] stories, myths, legends, and metaphors" (p. 282). They quote Selznick:

> Successful myths are never merely cynical or manipulative....
> To be effective, the projected myth must not be restricted to holi-

day speeches or to testimony before legislative committees. It requires some interpreting and the making of many diverse day-to-day decisions. The myth helps to fulfill the need. Not the least important, we can hope that the myth will contribute to the unified sense of mission and thereby to the harmony of the whole. In the end, whatever the source, myths are institution builders. The art of creative leadership is the art of institution building, the reworking of human and technological materials to fashion an organism that embodies new and enduring values. (p. 282)

One of the central themes of this book is that one cannot build a strong sense of community without a consensus formed around core values. A high school without them may have all the appearances of educating youth; but on closer examination, that education often lacks any real substance. Many excellent corporations obviously believe that it is possible to imbue their businesses with values around which all of their employees will rally. We need to test whether such an orientation is feasible in large high schools; and if so, we need to learn how to determine and then instill such values. Otherwise we should consider abandoning large high schools as unworkable institutions, as tens of thousands already have done each year by dropping out or by transferring to private schools.

Whatever values to which a school aspires, they must be hammered out through discussions among all the stakeholders: students, parents, teachers, and administrators. None of these groups should dominate the process if something more than a limited — and limiting — consensus is to occur.

These values are not goals or objectives such as one might find in curriculum guides. Values give direction, and each school can take many paths to express its values. While few in number, the values represent a litmus test for everything that is done in the school. New teachers and students are socialized in such a way that they know and accept these fundamental values. Values should convey big ideas like freedom and responsibility. These values must instill ownership and pride in the whole school. They must inspire and guide.

Stick to the Knitting. The meaning of this phrase is, of course, do what you do best. Stay with the basic business that has brought you where you are and avoid business you know nothing about.

Usually, criticism of high schools is coupled with an exhortation to get "back to the basics." High schools have tried for a long time to be all things to all people. They certainly attend to more than the basics by anyone's definition. The situation is further confounded by the many

89

publics who are continually defining and redefining what should be taught in the high school. Recently, many state legislatures have extended requirements in the major subject areas. Earlier, many of them mandated driver education. According to *A Nation at Risk* (1983), computing has become a new "basic," and many legislatures have now added it to their long list of "musts" for the schools. As always, sticking to the knitting in many schools has involved shearing the sheep, spinning the wool, dyeing it, and even crafting knitting needles.

One way to think about sticking to the knitting is to remind the public that some things are more important than others. Writing is more important than grammar. Problem solving is more important than rote memorization of math facts. Each community must determine for itself what these "basics" are. When the community is small — the parents, students, and teachers of a small high school, for example — the task is much more doable.

While high schools must learn to stick to their knitting, they must do so with some degree of caution lest they become even more inflexible in dealing with individual students. No one would think of knitting the same sweater for everyone. Neither should high schools become so focused on the "basics," by whomever's definition, that they offer the same curriculum to all students. What is needed is a focus on important aspects of the curriculum, determined by the community, and on flexibility in responding to the needs of each student, determined by teachers and students working together.

Simple Form, Lean Staff. This principle is a call for parsimony. In a literal sense, this principle may not apply to high schools. Perhaps the very largest school districts may have too many people in the central office who spend their time confirming Parkinson's Law, inventing forms for others to fill out. But small- to average-size school systems today probably are not as top-heavy as they were a decade ago. Recent increases in school expenditures are not going to hire additional administrators, nor are they going to buy more teachers. Rather, much of this money is being used to finance increased busing of students and to cover the increasing costs of utilities and liability insurance. Clearly, the trend is for the overhead costs of schooling to increase at the expense of instruction.

In high schools the problem is less in having too many administrators than in an up-the-down-staircase atmosphere that keeps the memos pouring out of the principal's office. In such situations, leanness means a change in attitude rather than a reduction in people. Leanness means not wasting time on trivia, not frittering away one's efforts on matters of little significance. Principals, too, must stick to their knitting. Perhaps that is the most important meaning of administrative leanness in high schools. The best principals already know this; the others must learn it quickly.

Simultaneous Loose-Tight Properties. The subheading under which Peters and Waterman discuss this principle carries this description: "fostering a climate where there is dedication to the central values of the company combined with tolerance for all employees who accept those values" (p. i). The most successful corporations refuse to compromise their basic values. If employees are not in agreement with them, they are free to move to a corporation whose values they respect. But if they accept the company's values, the company can be more tolerant of them as individuals with their own interests, needs, and concerns. The company can be flexible (loose) in dealing with their needs.

Some of the reform reports, such as *A Nation at Risk* (1983), suggest a "tight" approach: establish longer school days, longer academic years, more requirements, and more homework. Excellent corporations are more likely to use loose methods to achieve their goals, such as using flexible organizational structures, asking for volunteers, granting greater autonomy to individuals, encouraging regular and extensive experimentation, fostering strong social networks, and emphasizing the positive in evaluating personnel. This may come as a surprise to critics of schooling who find more severe remedies attractive, but it is nevertheless true: soft procedures often are the most effective means for achieving tight goals.

Peters and Waterman's "tight" properties are represented by guiding values, concise paperwork, regular communication, and quick feedback. The focus is on the problem and how it can be solved. One of the tightest properties of all, according to Peters and Waterman, is one we already have discussed, a focus on what the customer wants or needs. Peer pressure is another aspect of tightness. In the best high schools, as in the best corporations, each person takes responsibility for maintaining the guiding values of the organization. Each person continually reminds the others of what is important.

Finally, quality is the most important value in successful companies. If it did not produce high quality products and services, even the largest corporations would soon be out of business. Most high schools probably do not take enough pride in the quality of their products, their graduates. They need to use positive feedback to inform students of their progress toward high goals. According to Peters and Waterman:

> The nature of the rules is crucial here. The "rules" in excellent companies have a positive cast. They deal with quality, service, innovation and experimentation. Their focus is on building, expanding, the opposite of restraining; whereas more companies concentrate on controlling, limiting, constraint. We do not seem to understand that rules can reinforce positive traits as well as discourage negative areas, and that the former kind are far more effective. (pp. 322-23)

The principle of using positive feedback can apply to high schools, too.

> *Item:* The teachers and principals in a large high school agreed to use only positive terms in talking with each other and with students for one day. At the end of that day, spirits were high. Teachers went home feeling good. The students had responded in a more positive manner. The whole atmosphere of the school changed to everyone's benefit.

What if this faculty decided to make this practice a guiding principle every day? What a difference that one change would make in the daily lives of students and teachers! If the most successful corporations can run their businesses this way, we believe high schools can, too.

The Importance of People

Most of the ideas we have just discussed are people-oriented. They do not involve changes in technology, changes in the curriculum, or changes in training. For these reasons, building a sense of community in a high school is at the heart of our recommendations. It provides one of those central values needed for organizational success. It also provides the leverage for other people-oriented changes. When the people who inhabit large high schools learn again how important they are to the life of the school, when they are given the autonomy to make the changes that are important to them, high schools will become better places in which to teach and learn.

It is possible that this transformation can be accomplished in some large high schools, but we are very uncertain. We *know* that it can be accomplished in small high schools because we have experienced this sense of community repeatedly in our visits to them. In the next chapter, we will describe how one of these schools assembles the many concepts we have discussed here into a coherent whole.

Chapter 6
Mountain Open High School: A Model

Only if new institutions resist the temptation to direct them-selves principally to teaching the child can they fruitfully redirect their goals. One of these goals must be the development of strategies for coping with an information-rich and institu-tionally complex society; another must be the use of external activities where children are not students but contributors to a larger enterprise. Working with others under the discipline imposed by a common task and purpose is incompatible with the wholly individualistic goal of learning around which cur-rent schools are organized. And such involvement is necessary to provide both a direction to life and the motivation to learn how to implement it.

— James Coleman (1972, p. 75)

It's a real logical way to have a school.

—a Mountain Open student

What might a high school look like that combines many of the proposals made in this book? Can such a school function effectively on the funds typically available for public education? Can a small teach-ing staff — even a talented and energetic one — offer a rigorous, com-prehensive academic program to its students? Such questions can be answered by visiting a number of high schools throughout the United States. One of these is tucked away in a western corner of sprawling Jefferson County, Colorado.

Thirty miles west and 2,000 feet above Denver is the mountain hamlet of Evergreen. Resembling a model railroader's village, this community's businesses and residences are crammed tightly together, even on top of one another. But Evergreen is real. The number of Porsches and BMW's seen is evidence of how this once isolated village has become an affluent bedroom community of Denver in recent years. Evergreen also contains a very real school. Formally named the Jefferson County Open High School, it is referred to affectionately by its 210 students and dozen or so teachers as Mountain Open. This small public high school, now in its second decade of operation, offers a truly remarkable program.

Idealism as Everyday Practice

What is most remarkable about this small school is its utter sensibleness. Mountain Open's staff has considered all of what research, theory, philosophy, and common sense tell us about the education of youth and has acted on it. Idealists, who argue long and eloquently about what education should be but isn't, suddenly find that the obstacles to overcome in achieving their vision of a school are not in evidence at Mountain Open. The kinds of compromises that Sizer's Horace must continually make in America's typical high school simply evaporate in the context of Mountain Open. Consider the following examples:

Grades. Research suggests that grades have little positive impact on most students' learning. In fact, they have numerous, negative consequences. Teachers and administrators may lament grading practices but absolve themselves of complicity by pointing to school board policies, entrance requirements of universities, and the demands of prospective employers. Mountain Open has eliminated all forms of grading. The final act of a graduating student is to spend several weeks writing and refining a 10- to 30-page "transcript" that documents his or her experiences and achievements, describes his or her goals for the future, and includes letters of support from teachers and employers.

Attendance. Mountain Open's teachers take attendance in class, but formal classes are only a small portion of a student's total program. Therefore, attendance becomes an important issue of negotiation in the school's well-developed advisory system. When a student and an advisor meet to work out the student's individual program, they also negotiate an appropriate method for reporting attendance. What is important is students' participation in their individualized programs, not their physical presence in the building. Advisors meet with each of their advisees at least every other week unless special circumstances prevent it (most students go on many trips).

Credit. Theorists and philosophers often decry that learning is segmented, that it is packaged in arbitrary units called courses for which one earns credits. For many students the goal becomes one of acquiring credits rather than engaging in personal learning. Their motives are clear when they ask such familiar questions as, "How many tests?" "How much outside reading?" or "What do we have to do for extra credit?" Mountain Open gives no credits. Participation in classes is only one of many ways in which students demonstrate achievement of the many accomplishments required for graduation. At Mountain Open, tangible accomplishments are the primary academic tender. No one graduates by simply putting in three years, by making only a minimal investment of energy, or just by being civil to adults.

Evaluation. Philosophers tell us that to become independent learners, we must be weaned from relying on "authorities" to tell us when a job is well done. While students find security in being told where they stand, they also remain dependent. Mountain Open uses self-evaluation with feedback from the teacher. When students complete a project, they write an evaluation. What went well? What could have been improved? What of value was learned? The self-evaluation becomes part of the student's "transcript." Mountain Open teachers' role in the evaluation process is to react to students' self-evaluations and to help them see facets of their experiences that they may have missed. The written evaluation and the teacher feedback are a maturing experience seldom provided in the typical high school.

Individualized Learning. Most educators view individualized learning as an ideal to strive for; but in practice, only a few trusted students have a small portion of their program truly individualized. At Mountain Open, essentially the entire program for every student is individualized. Each student selects a faculty advisor who guides the student in designing his or her total high school experience. One of only two required courses in the program, called "Beginnings," is designed to help entering students understand their strengths and weaknesses and to clarify their aspirations. The emphasis on setting one's own direction and providing evidence of accomplishments along the way prompted a recent graduate to remark, "This has got to be the hardest high school in Colorado to graduate from."

Arnie Langberg, Mountain Open's principal from its inception until 1986, says that youth today have six major burdens to cope with:

- *Family.* They must learn to deal with the typical strains of adolescence as they affect their relationships with parents and siblings, even in healthy families.
- *Economics.* They must acquire enough money to function comfortably in today's consuming youth culture.
- *Independence.* They must first achieve and then manage the independence that is so much a part of becoming an adult.
- *Transportation.* They must find means of getting around in order to exercise their new-found independence. This could mean acquiring a car or risking the uncertainties of hitchhiking.
- *Personal Achievement.* They must become really good at something — a major requirement for developing self-esteem.
- *Sexuality.* They must reconcile their emerging sexuality as they develop new relationships with peers and decide which of the many sex role models they will emulate.

Langberg sees helping adolescents to cope with these burdens as an important responsibility of the high school. He also sees students in most high schools as having a seventh burden: coping with an unyielding institution that the law requires them to attend. Mountain Open strives not only to ease these six burdens for its students but also to eliminate the seventh as a central concern.

The Sociopolitical Context of Mountain Open

To understand Mountain Open, one must know something of its sociopolitical context. The school is in the huge consolidated Jefferson County School District (Jeffco), which has more than 75,000 students, half again as many students as Denver. It includes areas ranging from the older urban residential neighborhoods of west Denver, to newer suburban bedroom communities, to rural ranch country, to small cities like Golden, to small mountain towns like Evergreen. Jeffco is not a particularly wealthy district. Its per-pupil expenditure level of slightly more than $3,000 places it about in the middle of the 15 districts in the Denver area.

The district is almost totally white with only a small number of Asians, Hispanics, and blacks, most of whom reside in the older urban neighborhoods of west Denver. The socioeconomic range of the district is extreme; coping with social class differences becomes a major challenge for Jeffco's 15 high schools (13 conventional high schools, a vocational-technical high school, and Mountain Open).

96

Mountain Open is an open enrollment school, drawing its students from the entire district. While about 40% of its students are from the mountain area, every corner of the district is represented in its student body. The imposing geography of the district is compounded by Mountain Open's remote location on its western edge. This creates major transportation problems for many students, some of whom spend more than four hours a day on school buses. That students accept this hardship is one measure of their commitment to the program. But accepting does not mean they like the long bus ride. Below are the lyrics that a group of these commuting students wrote and set to music to express their feelings.

School Bus Blues

I like my blankets in the mornin',
You can tell it's mornin' by the clock;
Awake, arise, and set my mind to roarin',
Cold feet take my head down to the stop.

A way off in the distance, the boat is comin'
To save us from the freezin' cold;
Don't want to ride that bus this mornin',
You know the damn thing just might explode.

Just want to get to where I'm goin',
Just want to get my business done;
Cold feet in my shoes give me the
Monday mornin' school bus blues.

Don't think I can take this ride much longer,
Hey bus driver, let me to the door;
The noise, the smell, the bumps are gettin' stronger,
Tomorrow, I'll be comin back for more.

Just want to get to where I'm goin',
Just want to get my business done;
Cold feet in my shoes give me the
Monday mornin' school bus blues.

The Students

The diverse mix of students who attend Mountain Open fall into four groups. The largest group, representing 40% to 50%, are those looking for a school where they can personalize their learning. They were performing satisfactorily in their prior high school settings but saw Mountain Open as a more appropriate environment for them and made the move.

> I love Mountain Open. I think it is a wonderful school. I know I'm going to learn so much because I'm already learning so much, and we haven't even started Pre-Walkabout Skills and Walkabout. Before when I didn't have a class I felt like I could sit around and veg out, and now I feel like I want to do something. I'm always writing in my journal or doing something creative like writing songs or taking classes. It's not hanging out. I've done my share of that. I think the way this school is, is just the best. It's a real logical way to have a school. (Sweeney 1983, p. 238)

A second group of 20% to 30% are dropouts or near dropouts from conventional high schools. In some cases they have rebelled against the arbitrariness and constraints that characterize large institutions. Their learning problems more often result from too little parental support than from too little intelligence.

> I started quitting school in 9th grade because I knew they couldn't do that to me. I knew I was smarter than the diploma. To me it's a hoax and thought control and all these other excuses so I just dropped out and lived on the streets and accumulated a lot of experiences and travel. . . . I came back to school for the Recording Studio. It's what I've always wanted to do and the other schools don't have it. I don't need to know History or Math. That's jive. I don't need anything that pollutes my sense of life, you know. We knew about this school from our friend for years and years. I was on the waiting list. I don't care if I get a diploma. I am doing Walkabout. This school is the thing. If I had been growing up in schools like this, I'd be three times as clear of mind as I am now. In regular schools, you have a cloudy mind because you don't know who you are. You come to a school like this and you become yourself because you have nothing else to do. (Sweeney 1983, pp. 238-39)

A third group of 15% to 20% might be described best as the academically stifled — students who are alienated by the manner in which learning is packaged in the typical large high school or middle school. They may, for example, wish to study one area in great depth but can find no way to do this in the standard high school curriculum.

> I am in this school because of experiential learning. When I was in regular school my grades were extremely high and it was extremely boring for me in the regular school. It showed nothing. It taught me nothing and I didn't believe in the teachers and the

way they taught. Another reason I came here is because I had a friend who went here so I came here and my first two years here I did extremely well. (Sweeney 1983, p. 237)

The fourth group of 15% to 20% comes from Tanglewood Open Living School, an elementary-middle school that shares much of Mountain Open's philosophy. Indeed, it was the Open Living School's parents, concerned that the type of education their children were receiving should not end with the ninth grade, who urged the Jeffco School Board to initiate Mountain Open in 1975. They were joined in their effort by students (and their parents) from many of the district's middle schools; they, too, were seeking a different type of high school education.

> I think from being in it, practically all of my life, I've pretty much learned the values of the school. The values are self-assertiveness, to be able to learn on your own, to inspire yourself. We try not to do things in the classroom but go out and find out where it's happening and experience it, instead of reading it and memorizing it. They try to teach the kids to be more independent but in a positive way. Like here at the school, some people come from a regular school and they use it in a negative way. They go off and ditch their classes and it just doesn't work for them. I think kids need to learn how to be constructive. (Sweeney 1983, p. 239)

Open Living School graduates are a very important group in Mountain Open's student body. They come to the school already committed to its philosophy and, as a result, aid greatly in keeping the school on course.

Parents

As in any high school, parents are an important — often underestimated — factor in determining the character of the high school experience. Mountain Open's parents fall into three groups.

About a third of the parents are knowledgeable and concerned about education. They are college educated, often professionals, who tend to be philosophically attuned to Mountain Open's program. In many cases, they had to talk their children into giving the program a try. In this sense, they are ahead of their children in identifying with the school's philosophy.

Another third of the parents are at the other end of the educational spectrum. They have not attended college; indeed, their children may be the first generation in the family to finish high school. Because of disillusionment with or alienation from the large high school, their children have chosen to attend this "strange" school. In this sense, these children may be ahead of their parents in identifying with the school's philosophy.

The last third of the parents fall between the first two groups. While they may be dubious about their child's decision to attend Mountain Open, they support the choice. Some in this group simply are not very good parents. Their children have no real family. Some of these youth, as well as a few others from more stable home environments, are best described as emancipated youth.

These demographics look quite familiar. They probably fit the profile of most American high schools. These parents likely contribute neither more nor less to the success of this school than do parents in most settings. Mountain Open is a school that has devised effective responses to the changes that have occurred in America's families; however, it does not attempt to make adults better parents. These parents do no more and perhaps less to help their children make the transition to adulthood than their parents did for them.

The Program

The program Mountain Open's staff has devised is a complex one, not easily condensed into the single chapter we devote to it here. Accurate description is made more difficult by the program's fluidity; small high schools with equalitarian governance systems sometimes experience major changes over even a few years.*

Mountain Open's program is an adaptation of Gibbons' Walkabout curriculum (1974), which uses the metaphor of the Australian Aborigines' rite-of-passage into adulthood. The curriculum is built on the premise that to have a real sense of accomplishment — a sense of

---

*Much of the following account is freely adapted from the school's self-report, prepared by the staff for the school's 1983 North Central Association accreditation review. Besides our own direct, but limited, observations of the program and our formal and informal interviews and discussions with teachers and students, this account also draws from several important documents provided by the school. They are an unpublished draft of Bert Horwood's ethnography of the school (1983), for which the data were collected in 1982; Mary Ellen Sweeney's dissertation (1983), which includes several chapters on the school; the graduation transcripts of Thomas Candlin, Kenny Durbin, and Christopher Jenner; and several other program documents and newspaper articles.

100

having arrived — adolescents must experience a set of real challenges that require them to function successfully in adult roles.

The Mountain Open program is divided into three phases: intake and orientation, where students are brought into the program and helped to make a good start; Pre-Walkabout, where students attain competence in 49 skills demanded of most fully functioning adults; and Walkabout, where students complete six major Passages or challenges. Because the program contains so many elements that distinguish it from the high schools most of us have experienced, we shall describe each of these phases in considerable detail.

Intake and Orientation

Any Jeffco student in grades 10 through 12 is eligible to attend Mountain Open. Current students make presentations about the program to ninth-graders throughout the district, thus gaining useful public speaking experience. Applicants are admitted in August on a first-come, first-served basis. The fact that students (and parents) *choose* to attend Mountain Open gives the school an important psychological advantage.

The Mountain Open experience starts with a series of information meetings and interviews through which students and parents learn about the school, and it learns about them. All new students immediately are assigned a teacher-advisor until they know the staff well enough to make their own choice. That few students request a change of advisor is an indication of the even quality of advisement among the staff. Indeed, advising, in its many permutations, so permeates Mountain Open's individualized program that the key criterion in hiring new teachers is that they are good advisors who also can teach.

The first phase of the orientation is designed to help students learn how the program works and what is expected of them; to become acquainted with other students; and to come to know themselves, particularly in terms of the kinds of learners they are. New students entering Mountain Open can easily be overwhelmed by the situation where teachers are called by their first names; where there are no bells, no P.A. system, no room numbers; where some students may be listening to music in the lounge. Their "disorientation" becomes the basis for their orientation to this strange school. From the outset new students are encouraged to question all of their assumptions about what a school is. This will prepare them for their major task, which is to create for themselves the school that ought to be.

For the first three weeks, one class occupies all the new students' time. Called *Beginnings,* this class involves attendance at the weekly governance meeting, visits to advisory groups, and participation in a week-long field trip either camping in the wilderness or living in inner-city Denver. (Both experiences are considered important; the school strives to have all students participate at a later time in whichever trip they miss in Beginnings.) New students are divided randomly into groups of 20 to 25, with two staff members and two to four veteran students acting as assistants. In these Beginnings groups, the first activities are designed to help them get to know one another and to develop a sense of belonging.

> [Beginnings classes are] neat and they broadened my focus on this
> school. I didn't know that a place like this existed. It helped me
> to get a feel of where I was at and the possibilities for the future.
> It takes a long time to see how the school works. (Sweeney 1983,
> p. 247)

Preparing for the city or wilderness trip helps bring each group together. Students are encouraged to share any apprehensions they might have about the environment in which they are going to live. Student assistants describe their experiences on previous trips. Staff members explain how such trips can help the students function more effectively at Mountain Open. Students are asked to write their expectations for the trip and share them with Beginnings teachers, who serve as temporary advisors.

Students are encouraged to keep a journal while on the trip; at its completion they submit a written evaluation that includes descriptions of important events, what learning took place, how the trip measured up to their expectations, and how they felt about it. Students later share their responses with each other. One student described Beginnings as "a boot camp for our school. It is a good orientation" (Sweeney 1983, p. 247).

A number of other aspects of Beginnings, though less intensive than the field trip, are equally important in helping new students become part of the school. First, to help new students learn to use freedom constructively, they are not scheduled for a half day each week during the first three weeks.

> The largest and commonest difficulty that students found in their
> paths was the relatively large amount of apparently free time. Stu-
> dents are expected to take on the activities, courses and workshops
> that will extend their skills, meet their needs and empower them

> to complete the Walkabout Passages. The drive to attend sessions,
> to organize work and leisure, and generally to make productive
> use of their time must come from the student. (Horwood 1983,
> p. 40)

At the next session of the Beginnings group, the students share how they used their free time. Being able to manage one's time is extremely important because the amount of unscheduled time soon will increase rapidly.

Another aspect of Beginnings is a set of exercises that raise students' awareness of their feelings and values, followed by discussions of moral dilemmas as they relate to their own ethical systems. One of these exercises requires small groups of students to reach a decision by consensus and, with the help of an observer, to reflect on the difficulties of this process. This exercise is designed to enhance both personal awareness and sensitivity to others.

Also, new students are required to attend the weekly governance meeting so they will have firsthand knowledge of its function in the school. New students are told about the power they have and how they can exercise it. Governance meetings cover a variety of activities. Presentations are made by students who have completed Passages or apprenticeships, by groups returning from school trips, or by outsiders who would like to share something with the school. Major decisions regarding the running of the school are made with each student and staff member in attendance having one vote. Announcements of important activities of the week are made at these meetings.

New students visit a different advisory group each week until they have seen all five. These groups, consisting of two or three teachers and their advisees, are intended to convey the attitude that the group shares responsibility for the individual. They also are designed to maintain a sense of belonging, which might be lost when Beginnings groups are dissolved. In these visits new students get to know staff members who might subsequently serve as their advisor.

The last activity of Beginnings, other than a written evaluation of the class, requires each student to design a program for the next six weeks with the help of a Beginnings advisor.

Some rather remarkable transformations occur in new students during Beginnings. The school's former principal, Arnie Langberg, speaks to the point:

> You can see the kids change in three days. There has to be something about the kids that enables them to respond so quickly. We

103

can't be doing that much in so short a time. I think it is mostly that we allow the kids to be themselves. Some schools start with a kid by figuring out what he or she doesn't know, what I call a deficit model. We try to do the opposite; we try to help them see what they are already good at. It's a critical difference.

The second required class at Mountain Open is called *Learning to Learn*. It continues the work of Beginnings, including attendance at Governance and advisory groups, but is somewhat less intensive. Beginnings groups remain intact and still meet on a regular basis, but Learning to Learn groups are shuffled regularly to encourage students to make new contacts.

Learning to Learn introduces students to the language of Walkabout. Their work at this level concentrates on acquiring 20 core skills of the 49 skills that form the Pre-Walkabout phase of the program (to be described later). Students cannot enter the Walkabout phase of the program until all the core skills are acquired. The 49 skills are listed below with the 20 core skills indicated by asterisks.

Personal Skills. Be able to:

* 1. administer first aid at the level necessary for a Red Cross Multimedia Card or its equivalent.
* 2. strengthen and maintain physical and mental health.
* 3. strengthen self-understanding and self-confidence.
* 4. clarify values and develop principles for making moral decisions.
* 5. develop a meaningful relationship with another person.
* 6. relate effectively to two or more different groups.
* 7. understand how to relate positively to the natural environment.
* 8. understand the need for and the problems of transportation.

Lifelong Learning Skills. Be able to:

* 9. read.
* 10. write.
* 11. compute.
* 12. memorize.
* 13. analyze.
* 14. apply acquired knowledge and understanding to a new situation.

104

Investigative Skills. Be able to:

   *15. design and execute an investigation, using the scientific method, which results in a demonstrable conclusion.
   16. understand the social, historical, and moral implications of science.
   17. demonstrate the ability to use the library and resource materials.

Consumer Skills. Be able to:

   *18. evaluate quantity in comparison to quality of goods for the dollar.
   19. understand the methods of making consumer decisions, including the use of consumer-assistance agencies.
   20. understand the idea of taxation as well as specific tax details.
   21. understand the idea of insurance as well as specific details of standard insurance policies.
   22. understand the idea of interest as well as specific interest details.
   23. understand basic legal documents, for example, contracts, warranties, bills of sale, etc.
   24. identify types of credit.
   25. evaluate choices in seeking housing.
   26. identify the medical and nutritional options in relation to mental and physical health.

Citizenship Skills. Be able to:

   *27. demonstrate community responsibility through a community learning project or its equivalent.
   *28. locate community resources.
   *29. cope with a bureaucracy.
   30. understand the legal system.
   31. identify community, state, and national issues.
   32. understand the how and why of governmental operations.
   33. understand and recognize the basic causes and effects of stereotyping.
   34. identify the basic principles of economic systems.

Career Skills. Be able to:

   35. analyze employment trends.
   36. prepare job application forms.

37. develop effective techniques for interviewing.
38. understand wages and the main aspects of payroll deductions.

Aesthetic and Recreational Skills. Be able to:

  *39. create something.
  40. develop recreational skills.
  41. develop geographical, historical, cultural, and political perspectives for travel.
  42. enhance aesthetic appreciation.

Family Skills. Be able to:

  43. understand alternative family structures.
  44. understand responsibilities of parenting.
  45. plan for long-range economic security.
  46. deal with family crises.
  47. develop family activities.
  48. understand individuality within relationships.
  49. understand family planning.

Early in the Learning to Learn phase, students are given copies of their evaluations of the city or wilderness trip and of the Beginnings class and are asked, as a homework assignment, to relate their own experiences to the Walkabout requirements by listing each core skill they believe they have acquired. Next, students make a self-assessment as to which of three levels of achievement they think they have attained on each of these skills.

1. *Exposure.* This level implies a clear understanding of the skill as a beginner, where one has been primarily an observer rather than a participant.

2. *Experience.* At this level one should be able to explain clearly the skill to another student; one has used the skill successfully one or more times.

3. *Competence.* This level implies self-confidence in using the skill; the ability to teach it to others; understanding it well enough to be able to find and use resources relating to it; the ability to continue developing the skill independently; and where appropriate, objective measurement of the skill level by standardized tests in math, reading, study skills, etc.

One method students use to record their claims is to add a summary sheet to each evaluation with a list of the skills acquired, the level of achievement claimed, and a brief justification for each claim.

The final step of phase one of the program is for students to seek validation of their claims by sharing them with the teachers with whom they have worked on the trip and in Beginnings. A goal of Learning to Learn is for every student to achieve at least one core skill at the competence level.

Students are next given their Walkabout notebooks, which include a listing of the 49 Pre-Walkabout skills and descriptions of each of the six Passages. Skills acquired outside the classroom, on vacations, and prior to entering Mountain Open are accepted if they can be documented and validated. Students are taught how to use these notebooks to record their progress through the Walkabout phase. Student assistants, working with each class, serve as models as they relate their own experiences of how to adapt one's life to Walkabout.

Creative problem-solving and lateral-thinking exercises, which encourage students to search for alternatives, are other activities of Learning to Learn. Individual staff members also offer short seminars on a variety of ways in which a particular skill might be acquired and provide a model for self-directed learning. Since students have had little experience in planning their own program, the model provides a welcome structure to the ambiguity they are experiencing. The model contains seven steps:

1. Dream, imagine possibilities.
2. Set goals.
3. Assess one's self and the situation.
4. Create a plan.
5. Explore, experience, study, learn.
6. Evaluate the experience (and perhaps return to Step 1).
7. Record (document) the experience.

Phase one also includes several tests that help students document their current level of competency in a number of areas of the curriculum. The student's scores on these tests are used to diagnose deficiencies and to prescribe remedies rather than to sort or compare students.

When students choose their advisors, they establish a continuing connection with the school out of which most of their program will evolve. Any schedule that is developed must be mutually acceptable to student and advisor, and it must include regular contact between advisor and advisee. At different points in the program, a student might request experiences that may seem questionable; but if the advisor is willing to defend these choices, the school will accept them. The staff has developed a trusting, though hardly gullible, perspective on students and their learning.

Pre-Walkabout

Once new students complete Beginnings and Learning to Learn, they enter the second phase of the program, Pre-Walkabout. By this time students have chosen their advisors and have begun to form a good working relationship with them. Students now begin a closer examination of their current skills, assessing their level of ability in each, deciding how to document their past experiences, and choosing learning experiences that will help them develop unlearned skills. The school has a number of programmatic elements in addition to formal classes that aid a student in this process.

Advisory System. To work effectively, Mountain Open's thorough advisory system requires continual communication between students, advisors, and parents. During the first conference, the advisor tries to help each advisee to assess his or her personal, social, and academic development. Why the student chose to attend Mountain Open and the student's expectations are discussed. Expectations may include what the student thinks will be done, what "ought" to be done, and what the student would really like to do. Then a meeting with the student, the parents, and the advisor is held to discuss each party's expectations and to establish procedures for future communication.

Informal and scheduled meetings with the advisor are supplemented by a weekly advisory-group meeting, in which issues of importance to all advisees are discussed. Advisors augment their information about their students at weekly staff meetings, a part of which is devoted to reviewing students' programs, sharing perceptions and observations about them, and making suggestions. A student stresses the importance of Mountain Open's intense level of advising:

> I think the advisory system is great, but it does need more time. It is a prerequisite of this kind of school. Without it, a lot of people would be bumbling around. (Sweeney 1983, p. 249)

Each student maintains with the advisor a portfolio, which contains the student's self-evaluations, supporting statements from teachers and others with whom the student has worked, and anything else that the student wishes to include. The student's semiannual self-evaluation is the means through which specific needs are reassessed, current achievements are documented, and thoughts and feelings are expressed.

108

A meeting of a student's support group can be called by anyone involved at any time it is deemed necessary. The group's membership includes the student, advisor, principal, parents, and others invited by the student. Support groups occasionally meet to help students assess their progress and plan methods for overcoming obstacles to continuing their education.

Emphasis on Skills. The theory behind Pre-Walkabout is that certain basic or general skills can be identified. The 49 Pre-Walkabout skills are the outcome of staff members', students', and parents' attempts to define skills that a person needs to function in our society. To establish competence in a skill, students provide documentation from at least one learning experience showing that they have used the skill at the "competence" level. The student's advisor and one other person must then agree that the student is competent in using that skill.

While the documentation process may appear cumbersome, it generally seems to work. Although many students speak of "getting the skills out of the way," the procedures used make it clear that the staff puts great value on skills acquisition as necessary preparation for Walkabout's Passages and for life. Students seem fairly comfortable with the three levels of skills attainment and generally are honest in assessing their own attainment of each.

In choosing learning activities, students first determine what skills they need to learn and then seek ways to learn them. Or students can choose experiences that interest them and then analyze them for the skills they require. Most students eventually use both approaches.

An unusual aspect of the program — one that distinguishes it from most high schools — is that it recognizes any and all learning experiences a student has had, not just coursework in school. Mountain Open's philosophy is that if learning is really a lifelong activity, all types of experiences should be encouraged and accepted by the school no matter what their context. As long as the student can document the experience and find a person to validate it, the skills gained are accepted as genuine learning.

The curriculum offers students many ways to develop skills. In addition to classes at Mountain Open, they can:

- take classes at their area high school;
- take college classes;
- attend the nearby occupational-technical center part time or even full time;
- take school trips;

- participate in Community Learnings (generally these are apprenticeships);
- work in the Skills Lab (for English and math skills);
- participate in one of the school's special programs, for example, Munchie Central (a volunteer food service), the Recording Studio, the Greenhouse, Community Service, or *Passages* magazine (published sporadically);
- take part in activities offered at the school, such as leadership, fund-raising, dances, hiring committees, support groups for other students, special events, advising group activities, etc.;
- teach a class at the school or even at other schools;
- work, either after school or sometimes during school hours (jobs are an effective way to learn many skills);
- do independent study; or
- do a Passage in one area, and by doing so also work on skills in other, related areas.

While these are the most common ways in which students work on the Pre-Walkabout skills, the list is not exhaustive. The faculty continually stress that no one is ever really finished with any of the skills and there will be countless opportunities in life to use these skills. Accordingly, students are encouraged to continue documenting their experiences with skills even after they have been validated as "competent."

Documentation. A major task for students throughout the program is documenting their skills. At first glance documentation seems complex, even overwhelming. With practice, it becomes more straightforward, even routine. Every learning experience in which a student is involved must be evaluated by the student; and it always must include a response from the teacher or facilitator involved. Students are expected to list each Pre-Walkabout skill on which they worked, explain how they did so, and then decide and defend the level of expertise achieved. For all school experiences, the teacher (even if it happens to be another student) responds to each skill, validating the student's work. If the teacher disagrees with the level of expertise a student has chosen, judging it too high or too low, the issue becomes a matter of negotiation. Often, the problem is that a student simply has not provided all the supporting evidence that is available. More than 30 ways of documenting skills have been identified by students. The 17 listed below were identified by one Pre-Walkabout class:

written evaluations	support statements from other people
pictures	a project or product
reports	letters written or received
workbooks	oral reports or recorded conversations
journals	video tape, film, slides
interviews	grades from another school (present or
notes	past)
essays	awards and prizes
test scores	demonstrations

Classes. Classes offered at Mountain Open constitute only about one-third of a student's education. The other two-thirds, or what might be called Mountain Open's "de*classified*" curriculum, includes advisory meetings, trips, apprenticeships, and other experiential pursuits such as Passages. Students spend a large percentage of their time in classes early in their programs, and class time diminishes thereafter. Classes that are important in helping students continue their preparation for independence, responsibility, and lifelong learning tend to be small, generally enrolling between eight and 15 students. They are informal, and often two or more teachers will team. Instead of attempting to cover a large amount of material, the emphasis is on understanding basic principles and on planting the seeds for continuing interest.

> I sat in on a number of classes in traditional subjects. . . . The students were right. The teaching was "in a different fashion." In all cases the [subject] matter, even complex abstractions, had been experienced in some way by the students prior to the discussion. The students themselves seemed unaware of it, but there was also a marked lack of dependence on a single book acting as a text. There were lots of books in use, but no one of them centrally defined the scope or sequence of the subject matter. Those limits arose from the students' reactions to the experiences orchestrated by the teacher. There was also a major emphasis in these courses, as well as in the less academically oriented classes I saw, on the content being arranged so as to pose problems for the students to solve. (Horwood 1983, p. 72)

Teachers take responsibility for imparting some common body of knowledge, but each student is expected to delve further into some aspect of the subject and to teach it to the class.

How can Mountain Open afford to teach and even team-teach such small classes? In large measure, the program's major independent-study component provides the necessary latitude. The school also has disavowed responsibility for most of the custodial function — knowing

111

where every student is every minute of the school day — that so preoc-
cupies most high schools.

The degree of autonomy given students is exemplified on Wednes-
day mornings when the teachers hold their staff meeting. Horwood
(1983) sought to determine what happens to a school when the
teachers are not present:

> I made several slow circuits of the school during the course of
> the morning, stopping to spend a little time wherever there was
> something happening and ambling on otherwise. It seemed likely
> that the lounge would be heavily populated in the absence of the
> teachers, but it had no more action than usual. There were vary-
> ing numbers of people (from five to fifteen) using it during the
> morning. In the gymnasium a brisk pick-up basketball game was
> going on initially but gave way in an hour to the International
> Dance Class, started off by a senior student and then taken over
> by the volunteer Community Teacher who normally offers it. Five
> students were to be found in separate individual nooks and cor-
> ners reading or typing. Some of these had come from the early
> basketball game. Other individually isolated students included one,
> ferociously dressed in biker's garb, in the Principal's Office collat-
> ing papers and another person working at tuning the school's harp-
> sichord, a task that had to stop once the Dance Class started in
> the neighboring gymnasium. There were two students develop-
> ing film in the simple photography center adjacent to the labora-
> tory. The smoking porch had a steady but small stream of patrons,
> as had the coffee and snacks station in Munchie. An instrumental
> group was setting up in the Recording Studio. The lunch prepara-
> tion crew was getting started.
>   Of course this does not account for all of the students, nor for
> all of the places they might be. A number would be involved with
> some community activity that day, and the senior students would
> be away from school on Walkabout Passages in any event. No
> doubt there were a number who were simply idle. The point is
> that, in the absence of direct teacher supervision, the school pro-
> gram was functioning in its usual way. And more, there was no
> need for protective or custodial supervision. In how many schools
> does the staff feel that students can be left unattended? (pp. 31-32)

The program also has become a magnet for long-term visitors from
various parts of the country and for community people who affiliate
with the program:

> One was a retired actuary who taught a "Math Lab" in which prac-
> tice and remedial work in mathematics was available on an in-
> dividualized or small group basis. The other was a retired soldier
> with extensive diplomatic experience abroad who provided tutor-

ing in foreign languages not otherwise available at the school. The third person I found in a corridor one day where there was a student-built harpsichord in the final stages of construction. He was sitting beside a student helping her work her way through the tuning sequence. (Horwood 1983, p. 20)

Trips as Curriculum. Trips are not extracurricular at Mountain Open; they are an essential, integral part of the program. Despite the many unusual characteristics we have already described, it may be the school's emphasis on trips that most sets it apart from other high schools. Not only are trips seen as an excellent vehicle for experiential learning, but an extended trip often proves to be a turning point in a student's life — reawakening one's joy in learning; establishing trust in self, others, and the school; creating an "ownership" of the school and of one's own actions; and buttressing one's self-esteem:

> On this trip, I faced the biggest test of my courage that I have ever faced in my life. A big dream for me has been to dive with a whale. Facing this dream, to make it a reality, took a great deal of courage for me. I had only one practice salt water dive previous to my dive with the whales. Although I didn't see a whale underwater, I knew by their sounds and energy that they were close. I feel satisfied in this and I'm ready to face my next dream and make it a reality. (Sweeney 1983, p. 255)

> This place is like a shot in the arm. It has power all its own. On trips, everyone is the same — dirty, cranky, tired, and hungry. You can relate to people as themselves. You can experience life. Trips are a really good thing as it's a good way to learn through traveling. (Sweeney 1983, p. 256)

Four different types of trips are part of the Mountain Open experience. First, the school offers the sort of one-day trips familiar to most programs. Most *day trips* use a bus or school vans, with the addition of cars driven by staff, parents, or other adults when necessary. A second form is the *short trip,* which lasts two to five days and involves staying overnight. The wilderness and inner-city trips for new students are examples. There is a maximum student/staff ratio of nine to one on trips of this length and longer, and parents or other community members sometimes participate as "staff." Transportation for overnight trips can be school buses, vans, public transportation, staff cars, or even bicycles or canoes, depending on the type of trip, the distance, and the learning goals involved. Economic and safety factors, especially on what were, for a time, regular trips to Mexico, often dictate the use of school buses.

113

Extended trips form a third category, adding a unique element to Mountain Open's curriculum. They may last for a month or more, and are themselves a "class." The pre-trip segment of the class may be offered as a short, intensive class or as a regular six-, nine-, or twelve-week course. These courses typically cover the following:

- appropriate academic topics (literature, history, biology, geography, foreign language of the area visited);
- logistics, route planning, transportation;
- diet and menu planning;
- physical training (when appropriate);
- training to use special equipment;
- cultural awareness;
- environmental studies/awareness (waste disposal, recycling, care of trails and campsites, etc.); and
- budgeting and group fund-raising.

Some extended trips involve travel to foreign countries. In these cases, special considerations include obtaining school district and administration approval, notarized permission slips, passports or birth certificates, appropriate traveling papers, and extra insurance on vehicles (if public transportation is not used). Every effort is made to keep student expenses down on all trips by using inexpensive but safe transportation. Also, most trips are scheduled far enough in advance so students can save money from part-time jobs and plan their schedules and budgets with the trip in mind. One teacher estimated that a seven-week (all of December and most of January) trip to the Yucatan Peninsula to study the ancient Mayas cost each student only about $250.

Trips cost students so little because the school subsidizes them to a considerable degree. Where does it find the money? In part, it simply spends the same monies available to every high school in the country; but it spends this money in a different way. An issue we will discuss in some detail in the next chapter is the considerable overhead costs required to run a large high school. Mountain Open is one small school that does not have some of these expenses — particularly the expenses of a major interscholastic athletic program. The school negotiated with the superintendent's office to have these monies returned to it in the form of three leased vans and more than 50,000 miles of mileage money. Besides trips to the Yucatan and the original 13 colonies, these resources also have supported trips to Alaska, bicycling the length of California, trips to rural Mexican villages to perform community service projects, trips to British Columbia, and canoeing the Boundary Waters of Minnesota, to name a few. In a recent year, the school logged more than 77,000 travel miles on its three vans.

Walkabout adds a fourth category of trips to Mountain Open's program, *Passage trips*. When one or more students plan a trip as part of the Passage experience, they face a long list of required procedures before they can receive the support and sanction of the school and their advisors. In cases where students insist on taking a trip without receiving such approval, they are dropped from the school's rolls while on the trip and then may petition to be readmitted when they return. A Passage trip is approved based on the preparation and goals of the student or students requesting it. There may or may not be a staff member or parent present. All core skills and appropriate Passage skills must be documented at a competence level, and a proposal must be accepted by the student's Passage committee. The proposal includes but may not be limited to:

- a statement of major goals or major themes,
- a list of all preparations and previous experiences,
- knowledge of first aid at the level defined in the core skills,
- an outline of budget items and total costs,
- a time-line for each level of the Passage,
- a description of the types of documentation to be used,
- the "check in" method and the times when it will occur,
- personal contacts to be used as resources or in emergencies, and
- an explanation of how the student and committee will know the experience was successful.

Trips provide a number of academic, social, physical, and emotional benefits to students, which in turn benefits the school. They provide experiential learning in all academic disciplines. Students are motivated to continue classroom work back at school and in the future (self-planned trips, college); and they benefit from increased cultural awareness through visiting historic sites and by immersing themselves in foreign cultures, which helps to break down national and racial stereotypes. While on a trip, students have a 24-hour-a-day commitment to school. They also have a chance to break away from bad habits, family stress, and personal relationships and to see their life in new perspectives.

All students participating in a trip are expected to pay one-third of their transportation costs if school vehicles and private vehicles are used. Students and staff pay their own expenses for such items as food, lodging, and air fare. The school goes to considerable lengths to help students pay for trips through fund-raising projects, no-interest school loans, and job searches. Trip costs are kept low by sharing food expenses, seeking group rates, and often camping along the way with school equipment. Because of the benefits that extended trips provide, students are strongly encouraged to take part in at least one long trip before graduation.

Other Approaches to Learning. What Mountain Open terms "Community Learnings" has become a standard fixture of the program. Community Learnings offers students a chance to explore some of the many learning opportunities that exist outside the school. For some, it provides time to try out possible career choices; for others, it is a chance to learn from a master.

> In my younger grades at Open Living, I had a vet experience in 4th grade. In 6th grade, I worked in a grocery store. In 7th grade, I worked with a silversmith. By the end of that apprenticeship, they were buying stuff from me. It can be a hassle because transportation can be a problem depending on where you are doing your experience. It is an important experience and a good opportunity. It can broaden your horizons. It might make you decide to get into a certain profession. It helps you understand what is going on in your community. A lot of people are getting good stuff out of it. It can turn into a hobby too. I think it's important but not as important as school trips or Walkabout. (Sweeney 1983, p. 251)

One staff member's primary responsibility is coordinating such activities, including linking students who have specific interests with the appropriate people in the community. Each student who completes a Community Learning is expected to share the experience with others at the school. Often this requirement is accomplished by means of a presentation in Governance or in an advisory group meeting.

A second approach, "Community Service," involves students and staff in practical, productive service to local communities. The first exposure new students have to Community Service is during the city trip. Not only does each Beginnings class on the city trip do a clean-up or service project at the host site, but each student also is asked to participate in one of several Community Service projects for public and private organizations in Denver. These projects (for example, working in a soup kitchen or helping at the cerebral palsy center) are some of the most popular and fulfilling aspects of each city trip. Community Service projects are not confined to Beginnings classes; they can occur at any time in the program.

A third approach to learning uses the solar greenhouse, which the school built several years ago. A portion of the food prepared and served in the school's volunteer food service, Munchie Central, is grown there.

Mountain Open has its own recording studio, acquired through a federal grant. The studio has become the focal point for an unusual music curriculum built around the oral traditions of folk music, rock, and jazz. Students compose, arrange, perform, and record a variety of music. Masters are made of the best of these performances, and records are pressed and sold by the school to defray some of the costs of the studio. The curriculum has been adopted by seven other school districts in Colorado. The song, *School Bus Blues* (see page 97), was one product of this program.

Mountain Open's governance process is the heart of the school and deserves much of the credit for its continued success. This exercise in democracy begins each week with a Governance meeting, which is led on a rotating basis by students who have prepared for this responsibility by taking the school's leadership class. Attendance is voluntary. Students, teachers, and the principal each have one vote. Horwood (1983) describes one instance of the governance process in action:

> One attempt was made to modify the program during my visits. This incident so clearly captures the spirit and function of Governance in feeding the students' growing sense of power and commitment that I describe it now to epitomize the process. A senior student, not one of my interviewees, rose in Governance and proposed formally that some of the Pre-Walkabout Skills be removed from the compulsory core list and placed on the lists of prerequisites for certain particular Passages. In essence, the proposal rearranged the taxonomy of the Pre-Walkabout Skills and reflected a different value system from the one in use when the existing set of skill requirements was established. I was impressed that a student should initiate such a change and be taken seriously. There was a thorough and sometimes heated debate with about ten or twelve students and three or four staff speaking to the question. At the last, the chairman remembered that program changes must wait over a week and be publicized before taking a vote; resolution of the proposal was thus delayed. I had to miss the next meeting and my own denouement had to wait a fortnight. Then, I met the student who started it all in the lounge and asked how his idea had fared. He grinned and told me that it had been utterly rejected. I expressed mild surprise that he took it so cheerfully; and he replied that it seemed like a good idea at the time, but now he wasn't

117

so sure. Besides, last year he and some friends had successfully made a major program adjustment and you "couldn't expect to win them all." (pp. 54-55)

Like all deliberative bodies, Governance is often a messy, inefficient process. A student emphasizes the point:

> I think it's boring. It could be more exciting by putting less into it. Things could be said in a briefer way. Just a few people get some-thing out of it. Governance should only last 20 to 30 minutes. Only big issues should be discussed as it would make Governance more exciting. Announcements should be put in the minutes. I go about three times a month but that doesn't mean that I stay. Once a month I stay the whole time. It's a lot better than Student Coun-cil. In Governance everybody is involved and in Student Council everyone is uppity. (Sweeney 1983, p. 265)

Nevertheless, it is a critical factor in this school:

> Governance gets a lot done. Schools have problems because they don't have Governance systems like ours. All schools need it. I didn't have it until I was in the Open School. I go most Mondays because I'm usually interested in what is going on. (Sweeney 1983, p. 265)

To what degree every adolescent's education should include ex-periences requiring such involvement and commitment and demand-ing this level of independence is, of course, a philosophical question. That some students cannot cope with these demands, despite the sup-port of the advisory system, is to be expected. Lucille is one of the program's casualties:

> Lucille told me earnestly but in rather stilted language about the laxness of the Jefferson County Open High School program. She claimed that the school was very slack and that it did not provide the direction and structure that she required. When I asked her what had brought those facts home to her, she relaxed and launched into a long, laudatory description of "how much she had learned" at the school. She described the need "to be aggressive" not in an interpersonal sense, but in the sense of pushing herself forward into opportunities and experiences. She outlined her mis-takes, failures of motivation and responsibility in her first year and indicated how valuable those errors had been within the suppor-tive climate of the school. She told me how much more produc-tive her present semester was. All the same, those positive values were not sufficiently strong to impede her decision to seek a less challenging and more regulated pattern of education. (Horwood 1983, p. 42)

A teacher reinforces the point Lucille was making:

> I don't think any kid in this school can go straight through, safe
> and secure. I think they get pushed enough that that won't hap-
> pen. It's interesting to watch a student who is used to being a to-
> tal success. Because, of course, the tactics by which you become
> a total success wherever you were before are not the same here.
> The very best academic students are very threatened in this school.
> The rules have changed. (Horwood 1983, p. 83)

Walkabout

When students have completed the 20 core skills at a competence
level, they enter the final phase of the program, Walkabout. They must
now prove that they can use their skills in real-world settings. Students
are expected to develop ideas for challenging projects — Passages —
to demonstrate their ability to apply the acquired skills. The six Passage areas are:

1. *Adventure.* Involving a personal and meaningful challenge, the
pursuit of which requires courage, endurance, self-reliance, and intel-
ligent decision making.

2. *Career Exploration.* A broad investigation of a field of employment, including an in-depth study of at least one job within that field,
with particular attention to possibilities for the future.

3. *Creativity.* Develop a product that is an expression of one's im-
agination together with a detailed analysis of the process by which it
was created.

4. *Global Awareness/Volunteer Service.* Identify an issue having
global impact, followed by a study of how one's own culture and at
least one other culture deal with this issue, culminating in a service
project designed to influence the issue on a local level.

5. *Logical Inquiry.* An investigation that includes the generation of
a hypothesis, systematic data collection, and sufficient documentation
to allow replication of the study.

6. *Practical Skills.* Develop proficiency in a skill or set of skills that
one was formerly dependent on from others and that has the potential for lifelong usefulness.

The process for creating a Passage proposal usually involves:

- clarifying the idea with the advisor;
- reviewing a description of the Passage area(s);
- talking to the Passage-area consultants (two staff members special-
ize in each of the six Passage areas);

119

- writing a rough draft of a proposal;
- sharing the rough draft with the advisor, Passage consultants, parents, and other students;
- revising the rough draft into a final proposal;
- arranging a formal Passage proposal meeting, which includes the advisor, consultants, at least one student who has completed a Passage in the same area, at least one student who has not completed a Passage, and, if possible, parents;
- keeping notes at the meeting that will include all agreements reached in approving the proposal.

The staff tends to be less demanding of the first Passage than of succeeding ones; students who have successfully completed one Passage approach the next with a great deal more self-assurance. At least one Passage is done alone and at least one is done with another person or group of people. Students are encouraged to combine Passage areas rather than to do six separate projects.

In most cases, Passages are pursued away from the school; but students maintain contact with their advisors and keep them informed of their progress. Other committee members occasionally are involved, but the entire group reconvenes only for a Passage's closure. At closure time, the student's Passage documentation is reviewed, the experience is discussed, and its completion is celebrated in recognition of an accomplishment that is a tangible step toward adulthood. The student also is encouraged to make a presentation at Governance, which serves to interest other students about possibilities and gives the presenter some deserved recognition.

During this last phase of the program, the primary emphasis is on completing Passages; but students still are working on their skills. They also must create their final transcripts.

> [T]he writing of evaluations and transcripts is one of the most difficult tasks that students are called upon to do. They are not always done well. And they frequently form one of the commonest topics of discussion between advisors and advisees. (Horwood 1983, p. 30)

There are no rigid guidelines for the transcript; each 10- to 30-page document ideally reflects the individuality of its author. Generally, however, each contains a statement about why the student chose to come to Mountain Open, a brief description of the student's educational experiences, summaries of the Passages, and an indication of possible future plans. This personal narrative, together with supporting statements from the advisor and two or three other people with whom the student has worked, becomes the official school record that is sent to college admissions officers or other agencies.

When a student has completed the Pre-Walkabout skills, the six Passages, and the transcript, he or she is ready to graduate. Graduation occurs whenever the individual is ready. A final meeting of the support group is called for a personal graduation ceremony. The student's advisor, parents, principal, and anyone else that the student wishes to invite all share their appreciation of the student's growth as he or she reflects on the Mountain Open experience. The official diploma is awarded at this time.

Every program, no matter how tightly structured, has its "cracks" through which students may fall. Mountain Open has considered the possibility that a student might satisfactorily complete all 49 skills and the six Passages and still lack some quality that most people would deem important to a productive life. While such a circumstance has not occurred, the staff feels that it could; and the faculty and students currently are developing a set of "graduation expectations" that each student will have to satisfy either within the existing framework or in some alternative fashion.

Some students leave the school before completing the six Passages. In many of these cases, the student feels a need to "move on" to a G.E.D., military service, a job opportunity, or higher education. If a student has considered the alternatives and wishes to leave, he or she is asked to write a transcript; and if the student has completed at least one Passage, he or she is invited to join the commencement ceremony in June. Horwood (1983) describes the sort of unusual course that "dropping out" of Mountain Open can take:

> Other observations suggest that it is easy for students to move out of the school into the next stage of their lives. Indeed, this was exemplified in the extreme case in which a student on a Passage in a distant part of the world acquired other interests and dropped out of the school. Here was the student, in essence, completing the rite of passage independently and promoting herself into the adult community without benefit of graduation. (p. 57)

About 80% of Mountain Open's students go on to additional education, but only about a third do so immediately on a full-time basis. Staff and students offer three explanations for this pattern. First, a strong ethos at Mountain Open is "earn your own way"; students have been paying for a portion of their education (their share of trip costs), so paying for at least a portion of their higher education seems right to them. They often delay college for a time while they earn money for it. Second, the final sprint to complete the six very demanding Passages and to finish the last (often most distasteful) of the 49 Pre-Walkabout skills is very trying; many students are ready for a rest. Third, as one freshly graduated student put it, "Mountain Open students have learned to be purposive in designing their education." Horwood (1983) amplifies the point:

> I was struck by the presence, in every student interview, of statements that could only be construed as philosophies of education. All of the students commented on the processes of education they were experiencing. The students seemed to be aware of what the program stood for, how it worked, and what they thought of it. In one case, in describing an incident, a student related the behaviors of the people to Kohlberg's model of moral development. (pp. 81-82)

Students with this perspective are more likely to be purposeful in deciding when and where to go to school. They are less likely to simply go to college because parents or society expects them to.

Thus ends a student's career at Mountain Open. All high school experiences are important; but the investment that Mountain Open's program requires of each of its students would seem to make this high school education especially meaningful to those who experience it. As one teacher put it:

> We expect a fairly high level of ability to make commitments, to organize time and materials, and to follow through with things. To be responsible and accountable. I think we have high expectations about those things but we're frequently disappointed. But for students that make it, that get through and manage to complete the Walkabout program and graduate, I am just amazed at what wonderful people they are, and at how skilled and mature they are. (Horwood 1983, p. 83)

The Teacher's View

Teaching at Mountain Open is an unusual experience, as unusual for the teachers as it is for the students. Some of the differences for teachers from the typical high school can best be understood by examining four aspects of the teacher's experience: being interviewed and hired, establishing a workload, being evaluated, and being supported, especially during difficult periods.

The Interview. Mountain Open has a small staff with some turnover, but openings are rare. Those who wish to teach at Mountain Open face a number of barriers, especially if they are not already employed in the district. Jeffco's teacher association, like many of its counterparts across the country, has negotiated an agreement with the school board that gives teachers within the district preferential treatment when filling new staff openings. Such agreements assume that all the district's schools are essentially alike — a patently spurious notion for a school like Mountain Open. Openings first must be advertised internally, and eligible candidates must be interviewed. If no one proves satisfactory, the principal must show cause for not hiring any of the internal candidates; only then may the position be advertised outside the school district.

Candidates who make it to the interview stage confront their first experience with Mountain Open's governance system. Interviews are conducted by a committee comprised of the principal, two or three teachers, a couple of parents, and several students. All candidates are encouraged to visit the school before their interview so they will have a good idea of the unusual demands (and rewards) of teaching there.

Mountain Open has learned that being able to deal effectively with students one-on-one is the most critical skill for its teachers. Accordingly, the committee looks for a good advisor who also can teach. All candidates are apprised that their interview will include a simulated advising session with one of the students on the committee. The adults on the committee withdraw from the interview for 10 to 15 minutes to give students some time with the candidate without adult interference.

The process seems to work. Only once since the school was founded have circumstances forced on it a candidate that it did not want; that experience was a disaster for both the teacher and the school. Candidates for positions at Mountain Open receive considerable instruction about its unusual culture. They, like students in Beginnings classes, have undergone something of a catechism. It is possible, but highly unlikely, for "unbelievers" to survive such a filtering process.

Establishing a Workload. Teachers, accustomed to large, control-oriented high schools where their time is tightly scheduled, find Mountain Open a revelation. First, they are asked to keep about one-third of their time unscheduled for student advising and for Passage committees and support-group meetings. Also during this unscheduled time, they can plan, receive calls from parents or community people, discuss an issue with another teacher, and occasionally attend to a personal matter. The schedule provides the flexibility that enhances their productivity as professionals. Having this much unscheduled time could be abused by laggards; but this is hardly the case at Mountain Open, where close, continuing communication among teachers in a problem-solving atmosphere demands that teachers be productive. Indeed, when staff problems do arise, they tend to be due to overwork, not to shirking one's responsibilities.

Another third of each teacher's time is devoted to the routine activities of running the school. Weekly staff and Governance meetings, paperwork, and trips fill much of this portion of the teacher's workload. No teacher-led classes are scheduled during staff meetings, which take a half-day block of time each week. The staff meeting begins with an "executive session," during which confidential matters about individual students or some staff problem are deliberated. Once these matters are dealt with, the remainder of the meeting is open to student participation.

Also, no classes are scheduled during Governance meetings. Teachers are not required to attend, but they know it is in their best interest to do so. Besides being a good model for their students, teachers realize they are in a minority and their views will be lost if they are absent.

The remaining third of each teacher's workload is devoted to teaching classes. Teachers typically offer two classes in each academic block. One of these is "formal," which at Mountain Open means that it resembles a typical high school class with sizable amounts of reading, writing, and even lecturing. Genetics, theoretical calculus, basic computer science, and foreign language classes usually are formal classes. The second class is likely to be "informal" with a higher student activity level, less teacher-centered instruction, and perhaps several day trips. Examples include Creative Housing/Shelter, a course in which students design passive solar structures, and R.U.R., in which students study a potpourri of topics from expressionistic art to robotics and science fiction. The R.U.R. class culminates in a production of the 1920s satirical play, *R.U.R.* by Czech dramatist Karel Capek. But even these more familiar classroom routines take on an unusual character at Mountain Open.

The "interest-driven" program at Mountain Open does create gaps in the curriculum, a weakness about which Horwood (1983) comments:

> The students emphasized the many and diverse opportunities the program offered. And the trouble of excess loading into the schedule seemed to be a reasonable consequence. I was therefore surprised when one of the teachers suggested that, despite the wide-ranging talents and willingness of the staff, there were important deficiencies in the subject matter available. For example, there

was no expert instruction in modern languages and no in-house access to industrial arts or other shop instruction.... A related problem described by another teacher was the tendency for classes to be offered in a rather piecemeal, patchwork fashion resulting in a lack of continuity for subjects requiring a long sequence of instruction and practice. Again, students seemed not to feel a lack in this respect. (pp. 78-79)

Many classes are built around trips. Travel is more than a welcome break from classroom routine. Trips usually are the motivation for studying the content of the course. For example, a crash course in Spanish is a prelude to the Mexico Work Trip, a class that emphasizes cultural exchange and service to others. The planning of schedules, food, housing, transportation, and budget becomes a group responsibility for the class. The real-life skills such preparations require, not easily practiced in the typical high school curriculum, are central fixtures at Mountain Open.

In part to accommodate all the travel that occurs, the scheduling of classes is quite unorthodox. The academic year is divided into six blocks. The first three weeks are used to get new students started. Returning students work on their individual programs, discuss with teachers the classes the staff will offer during the year, and perhaps plan a class they themselves will offer. The next 10 weeks are devoted to an "academic" block. More than 20 classes are offered each block in a schedule that adjusts to the format and content of the class rather than to a preset schedule. Students typically take two or three classes each academic block. The next three weeks focus on preparation for extended trips, which usually occur during the following three weeks. Trips do occur throughout the year, but these tend to be shorter in both duration and distance. Some trips may be taken in the summer; for example, three students and their teacher were the authors' overnight guests on a trip to the State Department and Nicaraguan Embassy in Washington. The trip was a part of the extensive planning required for a class the following year that would travel to Nicaragua. (The trip ultimately was judged to be too risky, and plans for it were abandoned.) The remainder of the academic year is divided into two additional eight-week academic blocks. These blocks still allow flexibility, accommodating classes as short as six weeks or as long as 12 weeks.

Classes at Mountain Open often are team-taught, and they are never graded. While they may require certain of the Pre-Walkabout skills as prerequisites, they are open to all students. Classes are small, typical-

125

ly having 15 or fewer students, and usually meet two or three times a week with each session lasting from 75 minutes to two hours. The resulting program is diverse and stimulating. Indeed, Horwood (1983) sees disadvantages in the school's rich set of offerings competing for the attention of students and staff.

> Sometimes the schedule for any day could be regarded as an exercise in distraction. Students did not specifically mention this as a flaw; they were very engrossed in their options. But a number did from time to time complain that they had to miss something because of the pressing need to be elsewhere at the same time. (p. 77)

This problem is, of course, common to most large high schools. The difference is that students at Mountain Open are confronted with choices throughout the year, not just when the next year's schedule is planned.

Evaluation. Mountain Open's teacher evaluation process focuses on self-evaluation. Twice each year, teachers consider how they are progressing, what is going well, and where they need improvement. They prepare a written self-evaluation, duplicate it, and distribute it to the rest of the staff. Other teachers, in turn, sometimes react to elements of the evaluation, offer suggestions, and support their fellow teachers' efforts to change and to deal with the problems of teaching in this unusual school.

First-year teachers undergo a much more thorough, formal review by the entire staff and the students, which includes a review meeting to which everyone is invited. In this manner, everyone takes responsibility for helping new faculty make the transition into Mountain Open's culture, as well as for maintaining a high level of instruction in the school. Any veteran teacher also may request such a review. Because of the demands each review makes on the entire staff, experienced teachers are asked to limit their use of the review process to once every few years.

Support. Teachers request staff reviews, not because they need someone else to tell them about weaknesses of which they are already aware, but because they need to view their teaching from fresh perspectives or they need a major dose of psychic support. Teaching at Mountain Open is often exhilarating, but it is not immune to stress. However, the stress at Mountain Open is very different from that experienced in the large, impersonal high school, because its teachers shoulder the

126

burden of the many problems their adolescent confidants bring to them. Teaching at Mountain Open is not easy.

Mountain Open differs from most high schools in the extensive support system it provides its teachers. The staff review is the most visible element of this well-developed support system. Also, weekly staff meetings offer a continuing opportunity to reconcile problems while they are still small. For example, problems arising from miscommunication are rare on a staff that plans together as much as this one does. And because its entire staff has good counseling skills, these skills can work as well with a colleague in distress as they can with a student. The school's teachers tend to view themselves as helpers, and that role extends to fellow teachers.

Another source of support for teachers is the school's principal, first Arnie Langberg and since 1986 Ruth Steele. Mountain Open's principal is really a head teacher who teaches an occasional class, has one vote at Governance meetings, leads a staff meeting only when it is his or her turn to assume this rotating responsibility, and undergoes the same evaluation as any teacher. By muting their authority, these principals are viewed as a source of help rather than just as an administrator. The principal can and does change an assignment or arrange a leave for a teacher if that seems to be necessary.

All institutions tend to look good when everything is going well. How they deal with situations that are going badly represents the real test of their viability and resilience. Mountain Open appears to pass the test with a deceiving ease, which hides the burden that all this caring surely places on its staff.

The Meaning of Mountain Open

As we consider the account we have given of this school, its overwhelmingly positive tone unsettles us. Have we given a balanced view of Mountain Open? Is it really that good? Horwood (1983), who has spent much more time in the school than we, also grappled with this issue. He, too, was concerned about all the "sweetness and light" he was getting in student interviews. To assess his interview data more objectively, he conducted a word count:

> The count confirmed my impression. Some sixty percent of the descriptive words used by Jefferson County Open High School students were clearly positive in tone. In addition to those were words whose usage expressed admiration, such as *weird,* or the words of positive magnitude, *big, intense.* All told these come to

127

about seventy percent of the words. It is also noteworthy that the second largest category (about fourteen percent) were words associated with difficulty in the work, like *challenging, demanding,* and *hard.* (p. 39, emphases in original)

A program such as Mountain Open's is inspiring. The support it attracts from community volunteers and visitors is one indication of its potency. Its success prompted an anonymous donor to give securities valued at $82,000 to the school. Interest from this endowment supplements a variety of the school's activities; for example, a student may obtain a grant or a no-interest loan of up to $250 to fund a Passage.

James Coleman (1972) described the shifts that have occurred in society in the century and a half since the schooling model we still employ was devised. For the young, 19th century agrarian America was action rich but information poor. Children often functioned as responsible adults by age 12. Telling children about a world they could not know through any other means was a very necessary activity. A boy of the 1870s in rural Illinois could be awestruck as his teacher described a ride on a train that traveled 60 miles an hour. Now we have been transformed into an information rich, activity poor society, which has not been matched by a change in our schools.

> The school of the future must focus on those activities that in the past have largely been accomplished outside of school: first, productive action with responsibilities that affect the welfare of others, to develop the child's ability to function as a responsible and productive adult; and second, the development of strategies for making use of the information richness and the information processing capabilities of the environment. The activities that have been central to the school's functioning, such as expansion of students' factual knowledge and cognitive skills, must come to play an ancillary role.
>
> It is not clear just what the shape of future schools will be, but they must not have as their primary goal the teaching of children. Anomalous as this principle may seem, it is the key to successful educational institutions of the future. The failure to recognize this principle is a major source of malaise in present schools. (Coleman 1972, p. 75)

Is Mountain Open an anomaly? A Mountain Open teacher speaks to the issue in her semiannual self-evaluation:

> I used to have an uneasy feeling that we [open school people] were hiding out in an anachronism, a piece of the Sixties that was left behind, that we and what we were trying to do might be relics of the not-so-distant past, relics that others found quaint,

128

but didn't take too seriously. I no longer feel that way. It now seems that the way we approach education — in helping individuals to discover themselves and the world around them, in helping them grow in awareness and self-confidence and to become increasingly responsible for their own actions — that this way of viewing education is a necessity for the future.

One looks for the magic that allowed this school to blossom in our troubled system of public education. There is, of course, no magic to it at all. There is no outlandish per-pupil expenditure or federal or foundation funding, no particularly charismatic central administration or visionary school board, no rarified forms of teacher preparation. Rather, this remarkable school came about from an unremarkable set of ingredients: a group of assertive parents and students who wanted something different, a superintendent and school board willing to listen to them, and a principal with some good ideas and enough political savvy to make them work.

That all these ingredients already exist in significant measure in hundreds of school districts across the country is a measure of how close we are to a significant reform of the American public high school. One should not be blinded by the dazzle of Mountain Open's exotic trips, its Walkabout curriculum, and its advisory system. One could argue that we need a thousand more Mountain Opens; we will not do so. The meaning of this school lies not so much in what it has become but in the fact that it *became*. It provides evidence that significant reform in public education is possible in many communities if we have the collective will to carry it off. In the next chapter, we will discuss the complicated process involved in amassing that collective will.

Chapter 7
Reasonable Questions: Plausible Answers

Few citizens really know what's going on in their schools. They settle for the familiar form and ignore the substance. The businessman who would neither copy any part of the high school's routines or structure for his own firm's training programs nor tolerate for his employees the work conditions that are standard in schools sanctimoniously takes part in pep rallies for the schools. The college professor who on principle would not stand for close state regulation of her classes of freshmen blithely endorses tight control on twelfth-grade instruction, and even assists central authorities with that standardized regulation. Hypocrisy? Not really. Just indifference. And the unwillingness to think hard and honestly about the process of education.

— Theodore Sizer (1984, p. 237)

Six rounds of reform reports over four decades have said much about the trouble with the American high school, but the high school's current malaise can be summed up by considering three key problems. First, today's high school is too big to work well. Second, its structure no longer works. Third, it has little sense of community.

Size. The high school is strained beyond its capabilities. The picture is clearest in high schools that are heavily populated by the most difficult students. In some schools armed security guards with walkie-talkies are needed to protect students and teachers. Sizer accepts this standard solution:

> Safe schools are essential, but in some strained communities may be difficult to attain. Expensive retinues of security guards, police, and aides, in school merely to protect students from each other and from hostile parties from the outside, are unfortunate but necessary. That they are visible and active, with their walkie-talkies blaring, is no cause for embarrassment. It is simply an unequivocal statement that this place will be safe. No other priority can or should precede that. Nearly all students and teachers value it. (1984, p. 175)

But guns, walkie-talkies, and metal detectors are not reasonable solutions to a traumatic problem; they are last-ditch attempts to make an unviable institution appear to work. They are an embarrassment. Imagine how much more effective schools would be if they could buy additional instructional resources with the funds squandered on the paramilitary personnel and equipment that have become essential to keeping some schools safe.

That small size alone has a dramatic impact on such problems is well documented:

> State commissions in California, New York, and Pennsylvania based part of their recommendations for creating smaller optional public schools on increases in absenteeism and crime. "The incidence of vandalism, fighting, and drug-alcohol offenses in school was directly related to size of school," according to a task force report on California schools. In *Violence in the Schools,* Michael Berger [1974] reports that the sheer size of urban schools is a cause of violence, and that there is an "almost total lack of violence in alternative schools." (Smith, Barr, and Burke 1976, p. 153)

A 1975 Senate subcommittee on crime and violence in the schools cited the success of small high schools in handling these problems and recommended the creation of many more small schools (Committee of the Judiciary 1975). These successes were achieved in small high schools that enroll primarily youth that large high schools have found "unmanageable." In fact, the evidence suggests that large high schools provoke antisocial behavior in some students.

Structure. For too long, we have blamed the people in the institution for its problems; but they are its victims. The conditions under which teaching occurs are becoming unreasonable; the demands of keeping order increasingly are taking time from instruction. While

131

many people blame teachers for the problems of the high school, the real problem is the structure under which teachers must work.

In small schools the environment supports the acts of teaching and learning. People can not only be heard, they can be listened to. Reasonable effort produces visible progress. The demands placed on teachers and learners once again are reasonable.

Community. The large high school cannot support a viable community. The size of the institution makes it difficult to develop a commonly shared set of values; it seems to promote antagonism more than cooperation. But shared values are important. According to Sizer, "A successful class is one in which students and teacher agree on what they are about and on the rules of their academic game" (p. 154).

We have discussed earlier the importance of community if teachers are to function as effective adult role models. But community also is important because it enables teachers to function as colleagues of the youth with whom they work. Their roles blur and merge as they work on tasks *together.* Large high schools inhibit the development of the familiarity needed for this collegiality. In other words, small, personal schools can respond more appropriately to the realities of today's information society than can the large, impersonal schools that were created for the earlier industrial society.

If our public high schools are to work, they will have to change or watch a steady migration of students and resources to the private sector. Successful schools such as we have described here provide models for change. Anyone who thinks that a ready clientele for such schools does not already exist suffers from the same sort of delusions that allow one to feel secure among armed guards, walkie-talkies, and metal detectors.

Recommendations

Throughout this book we have suggested fundamental changes in the way the high school is conceptualized, changes that address the three problems we believe are responsible for the high school's current plight.

Size. First and foremost, high schools must be small. But small size alone is not sufficient; educators must capitalize on the potential that small size brings to the schooling enterprise.

These new, small schools must be different from one another. Choice, reflecting a variety of educationally defensible programs, is both possible and desirable. The notion of the common school has been little more than a myth for some time; but care must be taken that these small schools do not become merely new embodiments of the large high school's tracked curriculum. These schools should differ in how they prepare students (instructional approach), in how they organize knowledge (conceptions of curriculum), and in how they approach education (philosophy), not in *who* attends them.

Instructional choices might include programs that are highly individualized, that use a behavior modification format, that emphasize out-of-school, experiential learning, or that emphasize a standard classroom/textbook approach, to name just four markedly different possibilities. Curricular choices might include programs that organize content around a great-books approach, that organize knowledge around a multicultural orientation, or that emphasize bringing all disciplines to bear on one major problem for an extended period of time. Philosophical choices might run the gamut from programs that organize as free schools to those that emphasize traditional values of discipline and conformity (including behavior and dress codes). The point is not how these schools are organized but that their organization and philosophy have been developed by their participants.

Autonomy. Second, schools such as these must be much more autonomous institutions than schools typically have been. These small schools must be given broad control; those affected by decisions should be the ones making them. Teachers must be in control of instruction. How much of that control teachers choose to redistribute to students becomes a philosophical question. How much to redistribute it to parents becomes a political one.

After size, no factor expedites the development of community more than an equalitarian governance pattern. Not only does it bring a new responsiveness to the school's program, it also communicates to every member of the school community that their views are important. Everybody is encouraged to identify with the school; and as a result, ownership of the program occurs.

Community. Developing schools as communities has been the central theme of this book. But building a strong sense of community, even in a small school, does not just happen. Schools that lack community may not even be consciously aware of what is lacking. Only after spending time in schools with strong communities does one realizes its importance. Until educators experience healthy communities in small high schools, exhortation to change in books such as this will have little impact.

133

But What About ... ?

Our proposals raise many concerns that require convincing and plausible answers. Rhetoric alone is not sufficient; visiting successful small high schools and experiencing them firsthand is far more persuasive. The following seven questions reflect the concerns. They are important questions; they deserve considered answers.

1. What elements of the typical current program will be lost in the change?
2. How can voluntary segregation resulting from free choice be avoided?
3. Will small programs such as these be cost effective?
4. What happens to the formidable investment that has been made in large buildings?
5. Can school systems cope with the shift of control from administrators to teachers?
6. How do we overcome resistance to such changes from teacher unions?
7. How do we respond to the resistance of those who charge we are destroying the valued rites and rituals of the existing high school culture?

Program Erosion

What elements of the typical existing program will be lost in the change? Depending on what one values, the loss may be great or small. The *appearance* of studiousness suffers in small schools. There is much less passive sitting. Unfortunately, education policymakers often value such passivity. Teachers with noisy classrooms are suspect; state legislatures debate how much time on task (some legislators even call it "seat time") they should require. That so much of what we see is only a reassuring illusion often escapes us. That so little is learned in these productive-looking settings is regularly ignored.

> [T]he Philadelphia teachers' strike [of] 1972-73 ... lasted eight weeks. Some schools were closed and others were open the entire time. At the end of the year, scores of students who attended full time were compared with those of students who were out the entire eight weeks. No significant differences in achievement were found between the two groups. (Jennings and Nathan 1977, p. 570)

Despite their pronouncements to the contrary, educators tend to think that what is taught is what is learned. Students pass their tests and move on to new material. Few would consider it fair to administer the same exam to the same students a year later and expect them to do well. Much of the material we teach is learned only long enough to pass a test on it; seldom does what we teach have the personal meaning for students that ensures it will last.

In small high schools less *appears* to be happening; students may not even be in the school building. In fact, less that is *testable* is being covered.

> *Item:* Mario Fantini tells the story of his family saving money for years to take a trip around the world — the whole family spending several weeks seeing all the sights they read about in all those textbooks all those years. But Mario's son would miss several weeks of classes. Whatever the educational merits of the trip, the principal was concerned that he would be missing "important" material.

In other words, Mario's son would not be able to pass the tests that were given during his absence. The illusion of learning was so strong in this school that hard negotiating was necessary for the boy to make a trip that would clearly be the learning experience of his life. At times, our obsession with the testable is carried to unusual levels.

More troublesome is what happens to learning that requires years of drill. Foreign languages and musical performance are two areas that regularly seem to suffer in small, informal high schools. (There are some successful small high schools built around a performing arts curriculum, but these activities are not standard fixtures in most small high schools.)

In part, the problem may be one of perception; the problem of teaching foreign language in any American high school may just be more evident in less formal settings. We assume a good deal when a discipline like a foreign language is learned in high school. A personal anecdote may illustrate the point:

> *Item:* One of us recently spent a family vacation at Disney World. The long waits for each attraction were passed engaging in the popular pastime of people watching. The crowd had a very international flavor; people were as likely to speak Spanish, Chinese, Japanese, or French as they were to speak English. That three family members with either modest or ancient training in Spanish could not understand the Hispanics about them may be understandable. That a son who had just received an A in a college French course, and who had three years of high school French, could not understand the French-Canadians is less so.

The illusion of education is often that, an illusion. When we think we have learned something by doing well on a test, we still may stumble embarrassingly when confronted with the challenges of the real world. Teaching foreign languages effectively is an American problem, not just a problem in small high schools. It is quite possible that small high schools do not teach foreign languages as well as do large high schools. If that is the case, it may represent the major trade-off against the clearly superior performance of small high schools in promoting independence, autonomy, responsibility, and self-esteem, along with at least comparable achievement in other subjects (Gregory and Smith 1983).

Voluntary Desegregation

It is critically important to ensure that every school has a heterogeneous population. Schools must represent their community.

> *Item:* A large city school system in Ohio requires that all small schools maintain at least a 60/40 racial balance. The district's population represents a 50/50 split. Schools that do not meet this standard have a year to re-establish the balance or they must go out of business.

Small high schools have been used by school districts to alleviate race, sex, and class segregation. Magnet schools have been established deliberately to combat segregation by drawing a heterogeneous population of students to attractive educational programs.

Racial segregation is a serious problem in our society, and schools are one agency that may help remedy this ill. Large, anonymous institutions are not well suited to dealing with such problems. But small schools are much more likely to respond effectively to social problems because they can develop a community where people are valued as individuals.

Cost

Will small programs such as these be cost effective? One need look no further than the Pentagon to understand that bigger does not necessarily mean more efficient. But schools have embraced bigness, at least partly because of the desire for status, power, rich curricula, and winning football teams.

Unfortunately, the myth still exists that large schools are cost-effective. But the sort of overhead costs that large institutions require simply to keep running contribute little to the school's charge: teaching the young. Whole classes of specialists become necessary, specialists that cost money; they become a part of the cost of keeping school.

A very public statistic that represents a gross measure of the cost of education is the student/teacher ratio. School systems tighten their belts by raising the ratio or improve the "quality" of instruction by lowering it. A more obscure statistic is what we will term the student/non-teacher ratio. For example, we interviewed the principal of a high school in Wisconsin with 1,800 students, and we asked him to estimate how many people were on the payroll but never taught a class. After accounting for administrators, secretaries, counselors, security people, nurses, cafeteria workers, and custodians, the total exceeded 50. In this Wisconsin high school, the student/non-teacher ratio is about 36 to 1. If the average salary of these 50 people is $12,000 — it likely is higher — this school spent more than $600,000 a year just to provide non-teaching personnel, more than $300 per student.

Even small high schools have support personnel, but they require far fewer specialists. Some of the needs of large institutions, such as full-time administrators, security guards, and even cafeteria workers, simply disappear. For example, students who "own" a small high school tend to throw less paper on its floors and pick more of it up; vandalism of the property is minimized, and fewer custodians are needed.

Joe Nathan (1983) describes the degree to which overhead costs in the form of specialists can run amuck:

> [I]n Chicago there are big differences among the administrative staffs of the Catholic and public school systems. The Catholic schools, with 250,000 students, employ 35 administrators. The public schools, with 500,000 students, employ 3,500 administrators. One hundred times the number of administrators, for twice as many students. Do the children in the Chicago public schools need all those administrators? (p. 61)

Even if these figures are off by a factor of ten, they describe an alarming situation. What might happen to American education if even half of public education's overhead costs could be diverted to instruction, to buying more teachers or better teachers or, as at Mountain Open, trips all over North and Central America? Small high schools cost more money only if one tries to maintain the large-school infrastructure that small schools render obsolete. If that infrastructure is abandoned, more of the education dollar can be directed to instruction.

Architecture

Winston Churchill was aware of how people and buildings interact when he said, "We shape our buildings and afterwards our buildings shape us" (Deasy 1974, p. 5). The changes we are proposing have architectural implications; but it is people, not bricks and mortar, who will make these changes occur.

Abandoning all the large school buildings erected in the last 40 years is politically unthinkable; there is, after all, a formidable investment in large buildings. Fortunately, very few of these buildings have been built in the last 15 years, not because of a change in educational philosophy but because of a drastically lowered birth rate. In addition, even the well-built high schools of the early part of this century were seldom used for more than 50 years. Their newer successors, often hastily constructed in response to the post-war baby boom, have little chance of surviving that long. In sum, even if we continued to use the administrative model for which they were designed, we would likely abandon many of our current buildings in the next two or three decades, about the same amount of time required to change radically our way of keeping high school.

In the meantime, large buildings could support several small, autonomous programs. In many high schools, that conversion is fairly simple; they already have some form of physical separation into "houses" or departmental "pods," each containing a cluster of classrooms and a common area. Such specialized spaces as physical education facilities, music rooms, laboratories, shops, etc., present more serious conversion problems. Such spaces can become neutral turf, shared equitably by all the programs in the building. The problems of using current furniture are more subtle, but still serious. One begins to appreciate the tyranny of the tablet-arm chair as soon as one attempts to use it for almost any human activity other than passive classroom learning.

Ensuring that each program has sufficient autonomy is difficult when small, differentiated programs replace one monolithic one in the same building; but giving an identifiable piece of the building to each program is most important.

Using a large building in this way is obviously a compromise. Many of the overhead costs of a large high school still are present, and some sort of building manager still will be required. This person should not be the principal; he or she should have no responsibilities for guiding programs but should simply keep the building running.

But using the existing large buildings to house smaller schools is only a temporary compromise during the transition to small, geographically dispersed high schools. Planning of the new places these schools will inhabit is critical. Their appropriate locations are defined by the nature of the programs they will house. Schools may be housed in converted commercial space in downtown locations or may be adjacent to such education institutions as museums, zoos, and colleges. Schools might even be located at farms, outdoor education camps, or in the midst of a major local industry. Invariably, these schools will be less isolated from the community. They will be physically a part of the real world for which they prepare their students.

Decentralization

Once central administrators no longer are absorbed with keeping schools as much alike as possible, many of their coordinating responsibilities will disappear. Also, schools should be small enough not to need a full-time administrator. Over time, the number of administrators that are needed will decrease drastically. The resources spent on administration can then be redirected to instruction.

Teachers are important for quality control. While school boards should articulate some fundamental principles, decisions about education should be made by small groups of teachers, parents, and students whenever possible. School boards will need to establish reasonable standards, but stakeholders in these small schools would control their own destiny. Models for developing this balance between the autonomy of widely dispersed "outposts" and the maintenance of a common standard exist. Deal and Kennedy (1982) point to the U.S. Forest Service as an example.

> [T]he U.S. Forest Service is an anomaly. Its divisions are scattered all over the country — often in remote areas — which makes formal supervision difficult. It's the perfect candidate for a fragmented organization, and yet it is probably more well-knit — accomplished with less formal effort — than many organizations or companies half its size. Rangers act independently but in accord with the service's mission. They are "beings in their own domains" who handle most situations as precisely as they would if the boss were looking over their shoulder. (p. 195)

A realistic strategy is to let many administrative positions disappear by natural attrition. The average age of teachers in many districts now exceeds 50 years; the average age of administrators is probably higher. Most will retire in the next 15 years, about the duration for which their services might still be needed.

Teacher Resistance

One irony of our call for small schools that work better for teachers is that teachers, as a group, will resist such a proposal for many reasons. One reason is that such a change also will bring significant changes to the power relationships teachers have developed, especially in the past two decades.

Teaching has adapted to the industrial model that has done so much to shape schools since the 1920s. School management has become increasingly centralized as schools have grown in size and complexity. Quite naturally, teachers developed a big-labor response to these big-management practices; and the AFT and NEA, as we now know them, evolved. This relationship between big management and big labor is symbiotic; big labor needs big management to justify its existence. As the Ocean Hill-Brownsville incident, described briefly in Chapter 5, shows, labor will undermine a serious effort by management to decentralize its own power base. The New York City teachers struck to counter the school board's attempt to alter the existing balance of power.

Small schools have developed in school districts with a strong union, and they probably will continue to do so. A number of strengths that develop in small high schools, such as the lack of specialization and lack of narrowly defined job descriptions, seem to be incompatible with many union concerns. For example, the willingness of teachers in many small high schools to "pitch in" and undertake tasks that are not part of their regular responsibilities is not common in big labor-big management relationships. But if the change to small schools is gradual and first involves those most ready for change, the conversion to small schools should be successful.

The School Culture

School personnel are not the only people who will resist cultural change. Students and community people also will resist because change threatens the important rites and rituals associated with the large high school. Any change effort that simply tries to eliminate particular rites or rituals is naive. They exist and are coveted because they fulfill fundamental human needs for achievement, recognition, and meaningful participation.

Sarason (1971) describes the problems of changing an institution as resilient as a school. He summarizes his observations with the old French phrase, the more things change, the more they remain the same.

Sarason also emphasizes the importance of understanding the culture before one attempts to change it.

> If the more things change the more they remain the same, it is because our ways of looking and thinking have not changed. This should not be surprising when one recognizes that the agents of change from outside the school culture are too frequently ignorant of the culture in which the change is to be imbedded, or if they are part of the culture, they are themselves victims of that very fact. (p. 236)

Existing small high schools, with cultures similar to those we have described as exemplars, are the most effective settings we can recommend for developing a new view of the high school. The teachers and students who become participants in them can have a major voice in shaping their cultures.

Small schools do not simply happen. They happen only when small groups of teachers, students, or parents — often all three together — work to establish them. Commitment is the key. Those committed to new school cultures can break with the past and make a fresh start with small high schools. In these settings, they can develop a school culture characterized by new, mutually shared beliefs and values. Small high schools have a record of providing teachers, students, and parents with the means of accomplishing this transformation. We need only take advantage of their capacity to do so.

Epilogue
Hard Choices for the High School

The characteristic "large" appears to be consistently descriptive of the less satisfying schools [we studied] and consistently not descriptive of the more satisfying schools. This is a characteristic that is modifiable. Perhaps it is time that we did something about it.

—John Goodlad (1984, p. 251)

The next decade will be most crucial to the American high school. Because of its inability to respond to the changing nature of youth and society, the high school's structure is strained to the breaking point. Already the structure has become ineffective for too many of today's youth; and it presents growing problems for teachers. The numbing frustrations these circumstances have imposed on teachers are captured vividly in the following transcript of a radio interview with a fledgling teacher.

> Joel Donnerstein always wanted to be a teacher. Last fall, he got a job teaching English in a tough New York City school. The conditions in his school were probably more extreme than most but his experience reflects some of the same frustrations that many teachers feel.

> Donnerstein: I didn't quit until I found the right reason, and the right reason for me was that no teaching went on in the school. I talked to everybody eventually and one of the turning points

142

was when I talked to a man who really was the last person I saw who was compassionate, and he told me that, sometimes, Fridays aren't even a relief to him because they are too close to Monday.

Interviewer: Would you recommend teaching to anybody at this point?

Donnerstein: If you have the call and if you relate well to kids, I definitely would, but ... we're talking about a job that is emotionally exhausting, that is physically draining, and doesn't pay much. I mean, how can you advise people to do that when nothing in society respects that kind of thing? (All Things Considered 1985)

Teachers always have been underpaid, but there always have been other rewards, as Donnerstein says, "If you have the call ..." But as teachers' effectiveness wanes, they lose the public's respect. Is it little wonder that few will choose to pursue a career devoid of both extrinsic and intrinsic rewards? A teacher related the following incident:

I work as a meat-cutter in the summer at one of the nearby butcher shops, and I don't usually tell them I'm a teacher. One butcher finally found out that I was a full-time teacher and his comment to me was, "Man, that's a dead-end job. You must be a real dummy." (Boyer 1983, p. 163)

Teachers have begun to abandon the high school because they can no longer *teach* in it. Given the current abysmal conditions of high school teaching documented in the studies discussed in Chapter 1, it is predicted that those who will enter teaching will be less talented and less committed. The high school's slide into impotency will continue, perhaps even accelerate; and at some point society will abandon a public high school that no longer serves the needs of its youth.

The large public high school has at least four paths it can take in responding to these pressures, none of which will be easy. First, the high school can yield to mounting political efforts, exemplified by the recommendations of reports like *A Nation at Risk*, and try to perform its task as it did a generation ago. It can tighten the screws on teachers and students and try to make them more "accountable" by some narrow definition of that term. Perhaps it can even devise ways to "expel" both students and teachers who do not meet some arbitrary set of minimum standards. In other words, it can continue to operate as though the high school's growing ineffectiveness is a people problem, not a structural problem.

Second, the high school can fight a holding action by tinkering with elements of its program and gamble on the chance that the gathering darkness will be followed by a soon-to-arrive dawn. This course suggests that schools concentrate on solving the problems that can be solved and define the unsolvable ones as "society's" problems. The old saw about rearranging the deck chairs on the Titanic is a not inappropriate metaphor for this course of action.

Third, the high school can take conscious steps to try to improve its sense of community and its support of people *within* its existing structure, with the hope that this course can pave the way for structural change. Various attempts to break large high schools into smaller "houses," for example, have had limited success. Typically, such structural divisions have not been effective because even these smaller units have been too large; and they have been established as an administrative convenience, not as a way to create supportive communities for teachers and students. In addition, these subunits have never had much autonomy or identity; socially significant activities such as sports, the Prom, musical performance groups, etc., have been bonding activities for the "whole" school.

Fourth, as we have argued in this book, the high school can create new visions of schooling that are better adapted to the needs of today's youth, teachers, and society. One can pursue this path and still conscientiously maintain the existing large high school as an option for the diminishing number of students and teachers for whom it remains viable. In other words, no one need be forced to attend a school with which they are philosophically incompatible. We are talking about an evolutionary process that will occur gradually, perhaps over a decade or two, not a revolutionary one that threatens the vast majority of those connected with schooling.

What we must do now is to encourage those who feel the need for change and to support their efforts. Assertiveness on the part of policymakers is needed, not mere acquiescence to political pressure or simple cosmetic changes that result in good public relations for superintendents. Public school policymakers must respond before dissatisfied citizens withhold their support to such an extent that an effective response is no longer possible.

A school that has become a community will look and feel different to the people who live there. All of the participants — both youth and adults — will sense the difference. The consistency of decisions and actions that results from a democratic governance model will maintain a new social reality. A sense of caring and commitment will begin to permeate the school. This sense of community will extend to the parents and public as well. The stronger it becomes, the greater its influence will be, not only in the school but also in the larger community. Those who graduate, retire, or just move on from such schools will take with them a very different sense of the possibilities of what schools can become. They may not settle for less in the new places they and their children inhabit.

References

Aiken, W. *Story of the Eight-Year Study.* New York: Harper & Brothers, 1942.

"All Things Considered," Interview with Joel Donnerstein broadcast on National Public Radio, 8 September 1985.

Barker, R.G., and Gump, P.V. *Big School, Small School.* Stanford, Calif.: Stanford University Press, 1964.

Benne, K.D. "Authority in Education." *Harvard Educational Review* 40 (August 1970): 385-410.

Bennis, W., and Nanus, B. *Leaders: The Strategies for Taking Charge.* New York: Harper & Row, 1985.

Berger, M. *Violence in the Schools: Causes and Remedies.* Fastback No. 46. Bloomington, Ind.: Phi Delta Kappa Educational Foundation, 1974.

Berlak, A., and Berlak, H. "Dilemmas of Schooling." Paper presented at the annual meeting of the American Educational Research Association in Boston, April 1980.

Bestor, A.E. *Educational Wastelands: The Retreat from Learning in Our Schools.* Urbana: University of Illinois Press, 1953.

Boyer, E.L. *High School: A Report on Secondary Education in America.* New York: Harper & Row, 1983.

Bremer, J., and von Moschzisker, M. *The School Without Walls: Philadelphia's Parkway Program.* New York: Holt, Rinehart and Winston, 1971.

Callahan, R.E. *Education and the Cult of Efficiency: A Study of the Social Forces that Have Shaped the Administration of the Public Schools.* Chicago: University of Chicago Press, 1962.

Carmichael, L.B. *McDonogh 15: Becoming a School.* New York: Avon Books, 1981.

Coleman, J.S. *Equality of Educational Opportunity.* Washington, D.C.: U.S. Government Printing Office, 1966.

Coleman, J.S. "The Children Have Outgrown the Schools." *Psychology Today* 5 (February 1972): 72-75, 82.

Combs, A.W. *The Professional Education of Teachers*. Boston: Allyn and Bacon, 1965.

Committee on the Judiciary, United States Senate, Subcommittee to Investigate Juvenile Delinquency. *Our Nation's Schools — A Report Card: "A" in School for Violence and Vandalism*. Washington, D.C.: U.S. Government Printing Office, 1975.

Conant, J.B. *The American High School Today: A First Report to Interested Citizens*. New York: McGraw-Hill, 1959.

Deal, T.E., and Kennedy, A.A. *Corporate Cultures: The Rites and Rituals of Corporate Life*. Reading, Mass.: Addison-Wesley, 1982.

Deal, T.E., and Nolan, R.R. *Alternative Schools: Ideologies, Realities, Guidelines*. Chicago: Nelson-Hall, 1978.

Deasy, C.M. *Design for Human Affairs*. New York: John Wiley & Sons, 1974.

DeCharms, R.; Shea D.J., et al. *Enhancing Motivation: Change in the Classroom*. New York: Irvington, 1976.

Dewey, J. "Dewey Outlines Utopian Schools." *New York Times*. 23 April 1933, page unknown.

Dreeben, R. *On What Is Learned in School*. Reading, Mass.: Addison-Wesley, 1968.

Flanagan, J.C., ed. *Perspectives on Improving Education: Project Talent's Young Adults Look Back*. New York: Praeger, 1978.

Flesch, R.F. *Why Johnny Can't Read: And What You Can Do About It*. New York: Harper, 1955.

Gibbons, M. "Walkabout: Searching for the Right Passage from Childhood and School." *Phi Delta Kappan* 55 (May 1974): 596-602.

Glasser, W. "A Talk with William Glasser." *Learning* 1 (December 1976): 28-29.

Goodlad, J.I. *A Place Called School: Prospects for the Future*. New York: McGraw-Hill, 1984.

Gregory, T.B. *Encounters with Teaching: A Microteaching Manual*. Englewood Cliffs, N.J.: Prentice-Hall, 1972.

Gregory, T.B., and Smith, G.R. "Differences Between Alternative and Conventional Schools in Meeting Students' Needs." Paper presented at the annual meeting of the American Educational Research Association in Montreal, 11 April 1983.

Herndon, J. *How to Survive in Your Native Land*. New York: Simon and Schuster, 1972.

Horwood, B. Draft account of Jefferson County Open High School. Kingston, Ontario: Queen's University, 1983.

Husén, T. "The School in the Achievement-Oriented Society: Crisis and Reform." *Phi Delta Kappan* 66 (February 1985): 398-402.

James, D. *The Taming: A Teacher Speaks*. New York: McGraw-Hill, 1968.

Jennings, W., and Nathan, J. "Startling/Disturbing Research on School Program Effectiveness." *Phi Delta Kappan* 58 (March 1977): 568-72.

Joyce, B.R.; Hersh, R.H.; and McKibbin, M. *The Structure of School Improvement*. New York: Longman, 1983.

Hout, P. Remarks made during a presentation to the annual meeting of the American Educational Research Association in Montreal, 13 April 1983.

147

Kilpatrick, J.J. "Corporate America Offers Sound Advice on Schools." *Louisville Courier-Journal,* 19 September 1985, p. A-11.

Lewin, K.; Lippitt, R.; and White, R. "Patterns of Aggressive Behavior in Experimentally Created 'Social Climates'." *Journal of Social Psychology* 10 (May 1939): 271-99.

Lightfoot, S.L. *The Good High School: Portraits of Character and Culture.* New York: Basic Books, 1983.

Lortie, D.C. *Schoolteacher.* Chicago: University of Chicago Press, 1975.

Lynd, A. *Quackery in the Public Schools.* Boston: Little, Brown, 1953.

Lytle, J.H. "An Untimely (but Significant) Experiment in Teacher Motivation." *Phi Delta Kappan* 61 (June 1980): 700-702.

Lytle, J.H., and Yanoff, J.M. "The Effects (If Any) of a Teacher Strike on Student Achievement." *Phi Delta Kappan* 55 (December 1973): 270.

McQuigg, R.B., and Smith, G.R. "Aspects of Leadership Development in Leadership Oriented Adolescents." Study in progress. Bloomington: Indiana University, 1985.

Naisbitt, J. *Megatrends.* New York: Warner Books, 1984.

Nathan, J. *Free to Teach.* Minneapolis, Minn.: Winston Press, 1983.

National Commission on Excellence in Education. *A Nation at Risk: The Imperative for Educational Reform.* Washington, D.C.: U.S. Government Printing Office, 1983.

National Commission on the Reform of Secondary Education. *The Reform of Secondary Education.* New York: McGraw-Hill, 1973.

Newmann, F.M. "Reducing Student Alienation in High Schools: Implications of Theory." Unpublished paper. Madison: University of Wisconsin, 1981.

Nirenberg, J. "A Comparison of the Management Systems of Traditional and Alternative Public High Schools." *Educational Administration Quarterly* 13, no. 1 (1977): 86-104.

Peters, T.J., and Waterman, R.H., Jr. *In Pursuit of Excellence.* New York: Warner Books, 1982.

Rutter, M.; Maughan, B.; Mortimore, P.; and Ouston, J. *Fifteen Thousand Hours: Secondary Schools and Their Effects on Children.* Cambridge, Mass.: Harvard University Press, 1979.

Sarason, S.B. *The Culture of the School and the Problem of Change.* Boston: Allyn and Bacon, 1971.

Schumacher, E.F. *Small Is Beautiful: Economics as if People Mattered.* New York: Harper & Row, 1975.

Silberman, C.E. *Crisis in the Classroom: The Remaking of American Education.* New York: Random House, 1970.

Singleton, S.; Boyer, D.; and Dorsey, P. "Xanadu: A Study of the Structure Crisis in an Alternative School." *Review of Educational Research* 42 (Fall 1972): 525-31.

Sizer, T.R. *Horace's Compromise: The Dilemma of the American High School.* Boston: Houghton Mifflin, 1984.

Smith, G.R. "Educational Change by Legislation." *Viewpoints* 48 (May 1972): 39-56.

Smith, G.R., and Gregory, T.B. "Five Ironies of Program: Contrasts in the Curricula of One Town's Conventional and Alternative High Schools." Paper presented at the Bergamo Conference, Dayton, Ohio, 17 October 1985.

Smith, G.R.; Gregory, T.B.; and Pugh, R.C. "The SAS Inventory: A Measure of the Extent to Which Alternative and Conventional Schools Meet Students' Needs." Paper presented at the annual meeting of the American Educational Research Association in Los Angeles, 1981.

Smith, G.R.; Walden, J.D.; and Weaver, D.F. "Teacher Evaluation Practices in Nineteen School Corporations in Southeastern Indiana." Unpublished research report, Maris-Proffitt Endowment. Bloomington: Indiana University, 1986.

Smith, M.B. *And Madly Teach: A Layman Looks at Public School Education.* Chicago: H. Regnery, 1949.

Smith, V.; Barr, R.; and Burke, D. *Alternatives in Education.* Bloomington, Ind.: Phi Delta Kappa, 1976.

Stone, C., and Wehlage, G. "Four Persisting School Dilemmas." *Action in Teacher Education* 4, no. 1 (Spring-Summer 1982): 17-29.

Sweeney, M.E. "An Exploratory Structural-Functional Analysis of American Urban Traditional and Alternative Secondary Public Schools." Doctoral dissertation, Portland State University, 1983.

Swidler, A. *Organization Without Authority: Dilemmas of Social Control in Free Schools.* Cambridge, Mass.: Harvard University Press, 1979.

Weisman, F. *High School.* Documentary motion picture. Cambridge, Mass.: Zipporah Films, 1968.

Weinstock, R. *The Greening of the High School.* New York: Educational Facilities Laboratory, 1973.

Wigginton, E. *Moments: The Foxfire Experience.* Rabun Gap, Ga.: Foxfire Fund, 1975.